NORTH IDAHO HIKING TRAILS

Sheldon Bluestein

Challenge Expedition Company
Boise and Moscow

ISBN 0-9608120-0-8

Published by the Challenge Expedition Company
Box 1852, Boise, Idaho 83701

Introduction

Northern Idaho offers tremendous opportunities for wilderness hiking. Four of the state's five National Forest Wilderness Areas, totaling some 3½ million acres and including the nation's two largest areas, are accessible to North Idaho backpackers. Another 75 backcountry areas with about 2 million acres were identified by the U.S. Forest Service (USFS) in its Roadless and Undeveloped Area Evaluation II (RARE II), with six of these recommended for wilderness. Almost all of these roadless areas are still wilderness, where "the earth and its community of life are untrammeled by man, where man himself is a visitor who does not remain."

Through these remote regions run more than 7000 miles of trails, trails that traverse habitats ranging from the low desert environment of Hells Canyon to the high dry ridges of the Salmon River Breaks, from the low moist cedar forests of Upper Priest River to the high wet glacial-sculpted peaks of the Selkirk Range. These trails range from easy jaunts along gentle rivers like the lower Selway to challenging scrambles on craggy ridges like Reeds Baldy. Some trails follow historic routes, such as the Nez Perce and Lolo Trails, while others may soon yield to clearcuts and become just a footnote to history. (These will have plenty of company—the Forest Service had 150,000 miles of trail in 1944 and only 73,000 miles in 1965. It is likely that the official figure of 7000 miles for North Idaho is far removed from reality.)

The wilderness areas these trails traverse are a national treasure whose existence must not be taken for granted. Forest Service projections for the year 2030 call for a doubling of timber harvest and a halving of dispersed recreation. The greatest impact of such all-out development will fall on the places not recommended for wilderness by RARE II. Areas like Meadow Creek, 70+ miles from the nearest U.S. highway or railroad, with critical watershed and wildlife values, with high recreation and low timber potential, are being roaded and logged. And of the six North Idaho areas recommended for wilderness status by RARE II, only one has been so protected as of this writing, three years later. Meanwhile, the River of No Return Wilderness Area (RNRWA) has scarcely been established, yet is already under attack. If Idaho's backcountry areas, the most extensive and highest quality wildernesses in America, are to be dumped on the exploiters' junk heap, then what hope remains for the environment of the nation as a whole?

As "hard' resources such as timber and minerals become more scarce and valuable, so will "soft" resources such as wilderness, wildlife, clean air and pure water. Since passage of the River of No Return Wilderness Act, the balance has swung to the hard side. Concerned hikers can do much to mitigate this trend. They can work to maintain the integrity of the existing wilderness system, and to make necessary additions to it. They can monitor development in presently roadless areas, and encourage true multiple use land management, management that imaginatively integrates dispersed recreation and resource utilization. They can work with groups that maintain forest trails. Hikers *must* practice minimum impact camping techniques, and they should be willing to teach them to others.

Idaho's backcountry is not just a valuable but an irreplaceable resource, the product of eons of natural development and mere decades of human tampering. Once it is gone, it can not be synthesized; once it is gone, no amount of money or good intentions can recreate it. It must be enjoyed, understood, and loved now, that we may better preserve it for the future. The Northern Rockies wilderness system was established during a period of affluence and leisure unprecedented in human history. Idaho hikers must use and protect this resource so that future generations find in their wilderness legacy a reflection of our time's abiding concern for the natural environment.

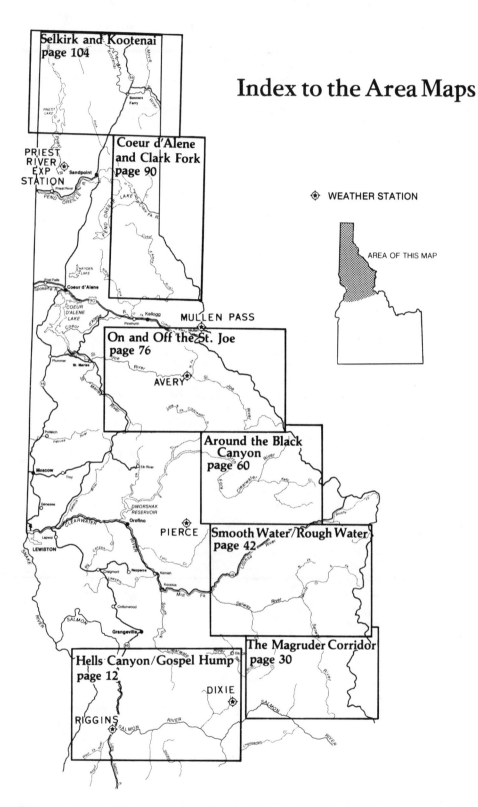

Index to the Area Maps

Selkirk and Kootenai
page 104

Coeur d'Alene
and Clark Fork
page 90

◈ WEATHER STATION

AREA OF THIS MAP

On and Off the St. Joe
page 76

Around the Black
Canyon
page 60

Smooth Water / Rough Water
page 42

Hells Canyon/Gospel Hump
page 12

The Magruder Corridor
page 30

PRIEST
RIVER
EXP
STATION

MULLEN PASS

AVERY

PIERCE

DIXIE

RIGGINS

PRIEST
LAKE

Bonners
Ferry

Sandpoint

Priest River

PEND OREILLE R.

HAYDEN
LAKE

Post Falls

Coeur d'Alene

Spokane R.

COEUR
D'ALENE
LAKE

Kellogg

Pinehurst

Plummer

St. Maries

Potlatch

Moscow

Troy

Genesee

DWORSHAK
RESERVOIR

Orofino

CLEARWATER

Lapwai

LEWISTON

Craigmont

Lawyers

Nezperce

Kamiah

Kooskia

Cottonwood

SALMON

Grangeville

SNAKE
RIVER

SALMON RIVER

Contents

This book is dedicated to Mary, who walked and drove many of these miles, and waited many hours.

Thanks are expressed to the Geography Department and its Cart-O-Graphics Lab, University of Idaho; to John A. Wiltsie for his generous help with the maps; to the Remote Sensing Laboratory, College of Forestry, U. of I., for air photos, advice, and patience; and to Myron Molnau, Idaho State Climatologist, for up-to-date climate information.

Wilderness Survival

Most people think of survival as a short term problem affecting a small number of people. Yet it is also a long term problem affecting the entire human race. Wilderness quality serves as a vital "control" on the variables Man introduces when he alters Nature's processes. When hiking you need to consider both aspects of the problem—can you survive the wilderness, and can the wilderness survive you? Do you possess the skills you need to protect both yourself and the environment?

Of course you must have adequate equipment to survive your wilderness journey. However, possession of the world's finest equipment does not guarantee safe backcountry travel. In a true survival situation, when the odds are tilted against you, you must count on the same piece of "equipment" that has enabled man to rise to mastery over his world—your brain. If you employ common sense you can improve your chances by: telling someone responsible where you are going and when you'll be out; carrying the Ten Essentials on all outings (see page 4); traveling in parties of at least two (although a party of four is safer, since a disabled person can be cared for while two go for help); knowing that three of anything—whistles, fires, yells—is the international distress signal; staying with your shelter in adverse conditions (since you can survive three days without water and two weeks without food); understanding that fear is a natural reaction to a survival situation, and that it can be channeled into constructive activity; and by knowing how to get found when lost in Idaho terrain. While going down most backcountry drainages will eventually lead you to a good trail or road, travel in brushy stream bottoms can be exhausting. It is much better to stay on ridgelines, where you have easier hiking and a stronger chance to spot the road or trail you have lost. Most Nez Perce trails followed ridgetops.

You must employ not only common sense but special skills to survive in the wilds. If you are a beginner, start your backpacking career slowly—these skills are not learned overnight. First read a book on backpacking. Try day hikes and overnight outings before attempting longer trips. Do several hikes at each level of difficulty before going on to the next. And learn the minimal impact camping skills described in this chapter.

In parts of North Idaho, especially the Selkirk and Clearwater Mountains, you must prepare yourself for possible encounters with grizzly bears. (The more widespread black bears can also act unpredictably.) One prime rule is that bears don't like surprises. In parts of Yellowstone Park, parties of four are required for wilderness travel, simply because four people make enough noise to alert bears. In high risk areas like Glacier Park, many hikers carry bells on their packs to give plenty of notice to grizzlies. If you do see a bear, give it plenty of room and don't provoke it. If you are actually attacked by a grizzly, climb a tree if possible, or play dead if caught. The odds are that you will never have bear trouble on the trail: bears like humans no more than humans like bears, and they keep their distance.

You *do* need to become skilled at safeguarding your camp. While bear trouble is rare in the wilderness, mouse trouble is common. You can expect problems each time you fail to safeguard your food: the only solution is to take precautions *every* night. Carry your food and cook kit in waterproof drawstring ditty bags, and suspend the bags from tree branches or nylon cords. Fresh foods such as bacon and fish attract trouble. Freeze-dried foods, much less odoriferous than the real thing, are a safer choice in grizzly country; and since they are easy to prepare on your stove, they eliminate the need for campfires, which also attract animals.

There are other critters out there waiting to get you, and you must be ready for them. The smallest are the microbes in contaminated water, and the worst of these is *giardia*. Beaver, sheep, humans, and horses have poor sanitary habits, so water purification is essential. The Forest Service urges that all water be boiled. The next problem critter in size is the tick. Idaho averages 16 cases of Colorado Tick Fever and 3 cases of the more severe Rocky Mountain Tick Fever each year. Untreated, these can be fatal, so early diagnosis is important. Symptoms of these tick-borne diseases appear in five to seven days, and include fever, headache, body ache, and a rash. The best prevention, especially important in the spring, is a daily tick check. The biggest problem critter is the rattlesnake. Logically speaking, Idaho has recorded no deaths due to snakebite in the last thirty years, and you shouldn't be too concerned about them. Emotionally speaking, you *will* be worried every step after you have seen your first rattler of the day. And while most are courteous enough to rattle and then move out of the way, a few rejects are either too dumb to rattle or too mean to move. If you are bit, remember that fatal bites are extremely rare, and don't go overboard on treatment in the field. The key to avoiding all three critter hazards is prevention — treat or boil your water, check daily for ticks, and watch for rattlers under 4000 feet.

Now that you have safely survived your wilderness journey, consider how well the wilderness has survived *you*. Have you adequately disposed of your waste? Have you left such traces of your presence as firerings where you cooked, fish guts and line where you fished, ditches where you pitched your tent, or cigarette butts and gum wrappers where you walked? Better yet, did you take care of all these things *and* carry out a bit of someone else's mess?

The Forest Service has perfected methods for wilderness sanitation and waste removal. For disposal of human waste, use a small digging tool such as a garden trowel. Select a spot at least fifty feet from open water (and well off the trail) and dig a hole six inches deep, to the soil's "biological disposal" layer. After use, fill the hole with loose soil, tramp in the sod, and camouflage the spot with pine needles. For disposal of camp waste, use your back or your fire. Cans, bottles, *aluminum foil*, and other nonburnables must be carried out. Burying is *not* satisfactory because animal or frost action will expose the mess. If you don't burn flammables in your campfire, you must carry them out.

Other guidelines have been established to minimize impacts on heavily used areas. They include a limitation on group size to twenty persons, a prohibition on limbing or cutting live trees, and a requirement that campsites be restored to natural appearance upon leaving. One important technique for restoring natural appearances is that for eliminating firerings. This simple skill should be applied whenever you make a fire where there was none before, or wherever there are too many rings in an area. When the ashes from your (preferably small) fire are cold, replace the rocks that surrounded it in their original setting with the blackened side down. Take unburned wood, ashes and charcoal and dump them out of sight. Then use soil, pine needles, and twigs to cover the fire scar. Results are impressive!

One tool works for the survival of both the wilderness *and* its users — the backpacking stove. A small butane or white gas model minimizes your effect on the backcountry. It reduces fire scars on rocks, nutrient losses to forest ecosystems, and risks of wild fires. It improves your chance of survival if things go wrong, for a quick drink of cocoa or soup can revive an exposure victim or give you extra strength to climb over a pass. It increases your enjoyment of the wilderness in marginal weather, when you can fix a hot lunch on the trail or a dry dinner in your tent. And it gives you tremendous flexibility in selecting campsites. You can camp where there is no firewood, or you can prepare a quick freeze-dried meal next to a creek in late afternoon. You can then fill your canteens and hike on to a high, dry, and wild campsite for the night. Purchase and carry a good stove! With one, you can truly camp and leave no trace.

Few Americans have been born and bred to be minimal impact campers. Most are products of the old bough bed, "campcraft" school, and some of the most strident advocates of the new camping ethic may have taken a lesson or two in its classrooms. But no matter how advanced your camping techniques, you won't be doing your best if you merely "pack out what you pack in." This slogan says nothing about the messes left behind by others. "Leave it cleaner and better than you found it" expresses the commitment to an untrammeled wilderness that every user of this book should have. Carrying out others' trash may burden your pack, but it will lighten your heart. If you follow this rule, then you will not degrade but rather improve our wilderness. And if you observe the common sense rules for survival, you will enjoy Idaho's backcountry for many, many years.

Equipment

Backpacking in North Idaho requires more sophisticated equipment than in other, drier parts of the state. The requirement imposed on you here, that you may need to hike on through days of rain, poses special problems. This chapter will make recommendations on sleeping bags, tents, clothing, and other essential and nonessential gear for North Idaho backpacking.

As Gerry Cunningham has said, the most important thing you can carry into the mountains is a good night's sleep. This starts on the ground, with a good foam pad or air mattress to cushion and insulate you. It ends in the air—the dead air space provided by your sleeping bag's insulation. This can be of two types, goose down or synthetic fiber. Goose down is still the champion for light weight, low bulk, high expense, and pure luxury. Its biggest drawback is its poor performance in a wet environment. After just two rainy nights, you will notice that your down bag has lost loft and insulating ability. Synthetic-fill bags have sharply contrasting qualities. They are heavier, bulkier when stuffed, less soft to the touch, and much less expensive than down bags. But they retain their loft in a wet environment, providing useful insulation in conditions where a down bag would be reduced to a heavy, shapeless lump of wet nylon. Whichever type of bag you choose, make sure it has temperature-regulating features such as a full side zipper and drawstring hood. A minimum comfort rating near twenty degrees should suffice for summer use—but remember that some people sleep colder than the Army troops on whom the temperature ratings are based!

In selecting a tent, you should take into account the wet North Idaho climate. A tent with a separate rainfly is almost essential. It should have a sewn in floor and mosquito netting door. Most campsites suggested in this book are below timberline and in the shelter of trees, so a high altitude/winter camping design should not be necessary. There is a direct relationship between tent size and comfort and tent bulk and weight: the more pleasurable the tent, the more painful it is to carry. But the chance of having to spend two or three consecutive wet nights in your tent should prompt you to buy one that provides some elbow and head room. Tarp tents or all-waterproof "backpacker tents" are not comfortable in rainy weather, when condensation drips down on your face.

You must have the correct clothing to fully enjoy the wilderness. You should be able to meet your shirt and pant needs with what you already have in your closet. Cut-offs or shorts are fine for some high country summer days, but you must carry long pants for bug protection, brushy stretches, and cold evenings. Many people hike in jeans, but lightweight, light color dacron/cotton pants are cooler in the heat and dry faster after the rain. While T-shirts may be adequate for some summer days, you must carry a good long-sleeved shirt for sun and mosquito protection and for cool evenings.

Some special purchases will be necessary in the outerwear department. The first essential is good raingear. While a poncho can keep you dry and double as a groundcloth, a rain parka with hood also provides protection from the wind and insulation for those extra-cold evenings when you approach record lows. Rain pants are needed for adding warmth on a cold evening, acting as armor against the mosquitoes, and keeping pants dry when busting through wet brush. The second essential is a goose down or dacron insulated garment. Parkas are excellent and can be used in spring and fall, but a vest along with a wool shirt or sweater is probably the most versatile combination for keeping you warm. Proper headgear is also a necessity. A wool hat will protect you from the cold, while a cotton sun hat will guard you against both sun and rain. Bandanas will serve multiple purposes.

Your miscellaneous equipment list is headed by the Ten Essentials for Wilderness Travel. They are:

> 1) Map. You should always carry a U.S. Geological Survey map of the area you are hiking. The maps in this book are intended as planning aids only: they are no substitute for a USGS map in your hand in the field.
> 2) Compass. Every once in a while, when you make a really huge mistake,

you will want to use a compass. At such times, it is helpful to have one!

3) Flashlight. One is always needed for setting up tarp tents in pitch dark and pouring rain. Penlights that can be carried in your shirt pocket are very handy.

4) Extra clothing. At the very least, always carry rain gear and spare socks.

5) Sunglasses. These are needed in all seasons, but especially in the spring when you may encounter snow.

6) Waterproofed matches. One effective way of protecting matches for an emergency is to seal two books with a plastic bag sealer of the "Seal-a-Meal" type. "Strike anywhere" matches often fizzle out at high altitude and should be avoided.

7) Candle or fire starter. Unless you have a real catastrophe when all your clothing gets soaking wet or your sleeping bag is lost, you won't need a fire — as long as you have a stove. If you must start a fire in adverse conditions, the Old Prospector's Method is to use the gas in your stove.

8) Extra food. An extra freeze-dried dinner provides a decent cushion for a weekend hike.

9) Pocket knife. The thinner the knife, the better. Thick knives chafe your leg and encourage you to carry heavy, expensive wine bottles with corks into places where Nature is so exhilarating that lemonade should suffice.

10) First aid kit. Consult your doctor or a backpacking book.

There are many non-essential items you should consider taking into the wilderness. They include toilet paper, the eleventh essential; insect repellent; suntan lotion; fifty feet of nylon cord; sewing kit; snake bite kit; a good book; binoculars or monocular, and don't forget that these can be used for close-up nature study when reversed; camera; a whistle, good for signaling distress; and gaiters, good for crossing bogs and creeks. An ice axe is an excellent tool for backpackers. It can prop up your pack at rest stops, serve as a third leg for difficult stream crossings, dig potty holes, and act as a cane to help you climb when your leg muscles have turned to mush. It can also function as it is intended, as a mountaineer's aid in snow and ice travel. An ice axe is almost essential for North Idaho travel over 7000 feet before July 4th.

Flora and Fauna

The area described here ranges in latitude from 45 to 49 degrees north, in elevation from 746 to 9011 feet, in rainfall from 13 to 65 inches, and in mean annual temperature from 37 to 52 degrees. These factors lead to a great diversity in plant life. Canyon bottoms along the Snake and Salmon are dominated by mountain mahogany, bitterbrush, and grasses such as brome, bluebunch wheatgrass, and Idaho fescue. At higher elevation southern exposures, ponderosa pine is encountered, and it mixes with and then yields to Douglas fir as elevation and moisture increase. Snowberry, ninebark, chokecherry, willow, and mountain maple form the understory of these forests. Along high ridges lodgepole pine yields to whitebark pine, alpine fir, and spruce, while menziesa, Labrador tea, and spirea are the common brush species. Western larch, grand fir, and lodgepole pine with beargrass-whortleberry understories occupy wetter northern exposures. Cool, wet valleys and mountains farther north in the state support forests of that most majestic and mysterious tree, the western red cedar, as well as western hemlock, western larch, and western white pine. The understory of these forests consists of pachistima, queencup, beadlily, bunchberry, dogwood, twinflower, fairy bells, and huckleberry. At higher elevations, subalpine fir dominates. The tremendous range in environmental conditions means there is a corresponding variety in wildflowers. Some of the same flowers can be observed in canyon bottoms in March and on mountain tops in July.

North Idaho is home to a great variety of wildlife. The larger mammals are moose, elk, white-tailed and mule deer, mountain goat, bighorn sheep, cougar, grizzly and black bear, wolf, coyote, bobcat and lynx. Smaller mammals include chipmunk, squirrel, marten, weasel, badger, otter, beaver, and porcupine. Toads roam the tall forests, while frogs are common in mountain lakes and ponds. Lizards and snakes are primarily residents of lower elevations, with rattlesnakes found in Hells Canyon, the Salmon River Gorge, and the Lower and Middle Selway River. A good bird list for northern Idaho is available from the Kootenai National Forest.

There are a number of nature trails in North Idaho that can help familiarize you with the area's plant and animal life. Heyburn, Priest Lake, Round Lake, and Winchester Lake State Parks all have nature trails and ranger-led talks and walks. The Forest Service maintains the White Pine Nature Trail 10 miles east of Harvard on ID-6; the Hanna Flat Nature Trail near Priest Lake Ranger Station on ID-57; the Bernard Peak Nature Trail at Farragut State Park (8½ miles long); and the Colgate, Major Fenn, and Ninemile Nature Trails on the Clearwater and Lochsa Rivers along US-12. The Bureau of Land Management has a nature trail in the Mineral Ridge Scenic Area, 7 miles east of Coeur d'Alene on ID-97. And last, the U.S Fish and Wildlife Service has eight miles of nature trails at its Kootenai National Wildlife Refuge, five miles northwest of Bonners Ferry on county roads.

Climate

North Idaho's climate shows a stronger maritime influence than the rest of the state. Only 300 miles from the Pacific Ocean, and lacking the Blue Mountains' rain barrier that intercepts much of Southern Idaho's moisture, the state's northern portion receives much greater rainfall. Most forest areas receive over forty inches of precipitation annually, and many high elevation areas get over sixty inches. The area's rainier climate and higher latitude are tempered by the lower elevations and warmer ocean air.

The Aleutian Low dominates North Idaho's weather from late September to late June. Cool, moist storm systems are borne eastward from the Pacific by prevailing westerly winds. Contact of these maritime air masses with the cold, dry air of the plains can result in short bursts of heavy precipitation, but most spring, fall, and winter storms are of low intensity and long duration. At last, as July approaches, the subtropical Pacific High moves northward and summer arrives in North Idaho. This is the period of thunderstorms, the worst of which are triggered when cool northern Pacific air meets warm, moist California coast air. Late August often sees a brief but intense invasion of this cool northern air that leaves snow on the higher mountains. September 20 is the average time for the abrupt transition back to cool, wet Aleutian Low weather.

Although both weather charts and climatic generalizations are included in this chapter, they are of limited value to the backpacker. What is crucial to him are weather forecasts for the weekends he plans to hike; these are best obtained by calling the National Oceanic and At-

month	mean high temp	record high temp	mean low temp	record low temp	total precip. (in.)	no. days greater than 1/10"	no. days greater than 1/2"
RIGGINS (1801 feet)							
Apr	64	95	38	18	2.0	6	+
May	74	100	46	30	1.7	8	2
Jun	82	106	53	39	1.7	3	1
Jul	93	110	59	36	0.8	2	+
Aug	93	115	59	37	1.0	3	+
Sep	81	105	51	30	1.1	2	+
Oct	67	95	41	16	1.4	4	1
DIXIE (5610 feet)							
May	56	81	28	4	2.3	9	2
Jun	65	88	35	20	2.9	7	2
Jul	76	92	37	23	1.2	4	+
Aug	76	94	35	19	1.4	4	1
Sep	66	88	29	9	1.9	4	+
Oct	54	78	22	-13	2.2	7	1
PIERCE (3175 feet)							
May	63	92	34	21	3.4	11	2
Jun	71	96	41	28	2.8	6	2
Jul	81	101	44	29	1.0	3	1
Aug	79	97	41	28	1.8	4	1
Sep	68	94	35	18	2.4	3	+
Oct	56	86	28	3	3.2	10	2

mospheric Administration (NOAA) office in your area or by listening to NOAA Weather Radio. You should be willing to adjust your plans according to the forecast. The hikes for each area in this book are arranged in order of ascending altitude. If bad weather is predicted, you should consider hiking a lower elevation, less exposed trail. A willingness to hike in bad weather (including the snow that can fall in any month) will earn you an extra measure of solitude even in heavily used areas. However, the solitude you experience while waiting in your tent for the snow to melt is not the most exciting type!

The charts that follow present critical weather data from five North Idaho recording stations. Most of these recording stations, pinpointed on the state index map on page iv, lie in valleys that are warmer and drier than the surrounding mountains. The stations' elevations are given after their names, and you can assume that the temperature is roughly three degrees cooler for every thousand feet of altitude gained above the valley. Differences in precipitation are less predictable, but you'll be closer if you add an extra 50% to the valley rainfall figures. The charts give the following information: mean daily highs and lows, the normal temperature range you can expect; record highs and lows, to give you an idea of how bad things can get; total precipitation, to provide you with an idea of wetness or dryness; number of days with greater than one-tenth inch of precipitation, to give you your chances of getting rained on; and number of days with precipitation greater than one-half inch, to tell you your chances of getting rained out.

month	mean high temp	record high temp	mean low temp	record low temp	total precip. (in.)	no. days greater than 1/10"	no. days greater than 1/2"
AVERY (2492 feet)							
May	67	95	39	25	2.5	8	1
Jun	74	100	45	31	2.3	8	1
Jul	84	107	48	31	1.0	3	1
Aug	84	111	48	34	1.8	4	1
Sep	70	105	41	24	2.0	4	1
Oct	55	87	34	11	2.5	9	1
MULLAN PASS (6022 feet)							
May	64	91	36	24	2.1	7	1
Jun	70	95	43	26	3.1	8	1
Jul	82	97	47	31	1.1	5	+
Aug	81	101	47	29	1.6	3	2
Sep	70	95	41	22	2.6	4	1
Oct	57	86	34	6	3.7	10	2
PRIEST RIVER (2380 feet)							
May	66	90	38	19	2.4	6	1
Jun	74	96	45	30	1.9	7	2
Jul	82	99	47	31	1.1	3	1
Aug	82	103	46	30	1.6	4	1
Sep	71	95	40	22	1.6	5	1
Oct	56	79	33	3	2.1	8	1

Geology

North Idaho's geology is tremendously complex. Out of this complexity has come the vast mineral wealth that made Florence, Coeur d'Alene, and Orofino famous in Western mining annals. The area still has great mineral potential, not all of which is outside of roadless areas.

The geologic record begins in the Precambrian Era, a forbidding 2 billion years ago. A few highly metamorphosed schists and gneisses remain from this Prebeltian time, and may be observed along US-2 from Priest River to Sandpoint. The major Precambrian rocks of Idaho, though, belong to the later Belt Series. Forty thousand feet of shales, sandstones, and mudstones were deposited in shallow seas that covered much of Idaho for 500 million years. These have been altered in the following billion years to argillites, quartzites, and siltites. In order from oldest to youngest, the Belt Series formations are the Prichard, Burke, Revett, St. Regis, Wallace, Striped Peak, and Libby Formations. The Prichard and Wallace Formations are the thickest, ranging from 8000 to 22,000 and 4000 to 10,000 feet respectively. The rocks were widely intruded by Idaho's oldest igneous rocks, the Purcell Sills. While most Belt rocks are located north of the Clearwater River, small pockets are also found along the Salmon River, most spectacularly as roof pendants in the Gospel Hump area.

The Cambrian Era saw a new sea, the Cordilleran geosyncline, cover North Idaho. The Gold Creek Quartzite, Rennie Shale, and Lakeview Limestone were deposited in this sea, and are best observed on the flanks of Packsaddle Mountain. Later Paleozoic rocks are virtually absent from North idaho, so this must have been a time of uplift and erosion.

About 250 million years ago, an arc of volcanic islands existed where the Seven Devils Mountains are now. The startlingly blue-green rocks found there are the product of Permian and Triassic volcanism that alternated with periods of sedimentary deposition. Among these sedimentary rocks are the Lucile Group limestones that contain Idaho's largest cave (in the Papoose Creek drainage just off the Seven Devils Road).

But the major event of the Mesozoic Era was the emplacement of the Idaho and Kaniksu batholiths, two closely related masses of granodiorite and quartz monzonite. The Idaho batholith covers some 10,000 square miles, from the Clearwater River south to the Snake River Plain, while the Kaniksu batholith is much smaller, restricted to the Panhandle area. Much of the Selway Bitterroot and River of No Return Wilderness Areas are composed of Idaho batholith rocks, while the Selkirk Range is the most notable example of the Kaniksu batholith. Emplacement of these batholiths took at least twenty million years, and when it was finished the rocks were not yet exposed – Cenozoic uplifting, block faulting, and eroding of older rocks were required to bring them to the surface. Much of Idaho's mineralization can be traced to contact zones of batholith and country rock. A road log for US-12, available from the Idaho Bureau of Mines and Geology, can be used to study the Idaho batholith in the Clearwater-Lochsa Canyon.

Cenozoic times have been notable for fire and ice. The Columbia River Basalts flooded much of North Idaho with lava during the Miocene Epoch, some 25 million years ago. Layers of stream and lake sediments and ash are interspersed between the basalt sheets. These rocks are best observed on Lewiston and Culdesac Hills. Pleistocene glaciation forms the most exciting part of the geologic story. Both alpine and continental glaciation altered the face of North Idaho. Huge ice sheets marched down the Purcell Trench from Canada, flattening the Rathdrum Prairie and creating Hayden, Spirit, and Pend Oreille Lakes. These glaciers dammed rivers, creating lakes in western Montana. Several ice dams washed out with catastrophic effects on Eastern Washington. In the mountains, glaciers carved the steep horns of the Selkirks, Bitterroots, and Selway Crags, and gouged out cirques that hold mountain lakes and meadows.

Mount Saint Helens wrote the most recent chapter in North Idaho's geologic story on May 18, 1980. It blotted out the sun over much of the region and deposited up to an inch of ash in the mountains. Some of this ash fell on snowbanks that, as they melted, concentrated the ash into little piles of "that grey stuff" which can still be seen on high ridges.

How to Use This Book

The remaining pages of this book contain information on fifty hiking trails in North Central and Northern Idaho. Selection of the trails was based on quality of the wilderness experience, ease of access to the trailhead, possibility of loop routes or extended hikes, and a desire to introduce hikers to the great variety in North Idaho's backcountry. The main features of each trail description are a list of key facts, including total distance, level of difficulty, season of use, elevation gain, maps of the area, and road mileage to the trailhead; an introduction to the area; a description of the trail; a discussion of extended hikes; and directions to the trailhead.

The first key fact is a listing of the types of hikes possible on the trail. A "D" indicates that a dayhike in the 4 to 9 mile round trip range is possible. An "O" means an overnight hike in the 4 to 10 mile range can be made. Such a hike might start in mid-afternoon and end at the same time next day. A "W" indicates that a two night, weekend trip is possible, in the 12 to 22 mile range. Trail descriptions are mainly oriented toward such hikes, which could start either Friday night or Saturday morning and end on Sunday evening. An "E" means that extended trips, from three days to three weeks, can be made. In most cases all four types of hikes can be made: but it is important that you know (for example) that there is no good campsite in overnight range, no good viewpoint in dayhiker's range, or simply nowhere to go beyond the weekender's goal.

The second fact given is the round trip distance of the hike. Usually this is for the weekend hike, and you read "Total Distance, W". Occasionally, this figure is for an overnight hike, so you will see "Total Distance, O". Please note that *total* distance is always given. Some hikes are loops for which a one-way mileage would have little meaning.

The third key fact is the difficulty of the hike. "Level I" hikes are well suited to beginners. Such trails are generally easy to follow, fairly level, and more soily than rocky. "Level II" hikes are best for people of intermediate ability. They are usually steeper, occasionally difficult to follow, and may have rocky stretches or stream crossings. "Level III" trails are for advanced hikers. They have stretches that are steep, rocky, and/or hard to follow. Some involve off-trail cross-country travel, while others present special problems such as lack of water or traditional type campsites. Many of the hikes start at a low level of difficulty and become progressively harder. These are noted as "Levels I, II", etc.

The fourth fact, season of use, is necessarily an estimate. The starting date can be two or three weeks off, since each snow year and each thaw is different. Advanced hikers can cheat on these dates and push the season if they carry ice axes and know how to use them. Your best policy is to check with Forest Headquarters for current road and trail information. The closing date is either the opening day of hunting season or September 20. It's no fun to backpack when bullets are flying and trails are clogged with hunters, and later travel risks severe weather. Please remember that these dates are only averages. Readers who treat them as gospel will be unpleasantly surprised from time to time.

The fifth key fact is the elevation gain for the hike specified under "Total Distance". This, too, is a round trip figure, since not all hikes climb to a high spot and stop. Rather, many gain *and* lose altitude on entry *and* exit.

The sixth key fact is the U.S. Geological Survey (USGS) map or maps that cover the weekend hike. Much of North Idaho is charted by maps in the 15-minute series (1:62,500 scale) or the 7½-minute series (1:24,000 scale). Most of these maps were produced in the 1950's and 60's, and they are showing their age. Unless otherwise specified, all maps are at the 1:24,000 scale. If a map's name is followed by an asterisk, it only covers a small part of the hike, and is not absolutely necessary for your safe travel.

Two excellent outlets for USGS maps are easily accessible to North Idahoans, saving them from the hassle of mail ordering. The USGS operates a map store in Spokane's Federal Building, while the Idaho Bureau of Mines and Geology (IBMG) in Moscow sells all USGS maps of Idaho as well as their own excellent maps and books. In addition, USGS map repositories are located at the University of Idaho (Moscow), the Spokane Public Library, and Washington State University (Pullman). USGS maps of the entire United States can be viewed. If you cannot reach the Spokane or Moscow sales offices, write the USGS (see page 11), and request the State Map Index. It gives instructions for mail ordering maps, and also has a listing of retail stores that sell maps. The seventh key fact is the U.S. Forest Service (USFS) map of the area. These come in four types. Forest Travel Plans give the widest coverage. These free maps show the Nez Perce, Clearwater, Bitterroot, and Idaho Panhandle National Forests, and give current information on road and trail restrictions. Larger scale Forest Maps can be purchased for the above forests as well as for the St Joe, Coeur d'Alene, and Kaniksu N.F.s (these three were consolidated into the Idaho Panhandle N.F. (I.P.N.F.). Free Ranger District Maps are widely available on the Nez Perce and Clearwater N.F.s. Special Area Maps cover wilderness and national recreation areas. The year 1980 saw a new map for the Selway Bitterroot and a preliminary map for the River of No Return Wilderness Areas. A Hells Canyon National Recreation Area map is due out in 1983 or 84.

The last key fact is the road mileage to the trailhead. The first number is the total distance, while the portion on dirt roads is given in parentheses. These mileages are given from either "CdA", the junction of US-95 and I-90 on the west side of Coeur d'Alene; or from "Lew", the junction of US-95 and US-12 at Spalding, eight miles east of Lewiston.

Following the key facts comes an introduction. It attempts to put the trail in the context of the area it passes through: what makes it special, how RARE-II rated the area, what its prospects are for the future. Then comes the trail description, which is not so detailed that you are constantly looking for the next landmark, but which does describe trouble spots along the way. The trails were field checked in 1980 and 81, and the descriptions should remain accurate for years, barring slides, floods, fires, and bulldozers. There follows a section on extended trips, most of which have not yet been hiked by the author; these have caught his eye on maps, air photos, or in the field.

Last come directions to the trailhead. The author hopes you never get lost on Idaho's backwoods roads. He well knows the feeling, and wishes it on no one! One problem is with automobile odometers, which vary in accuracy. If you don't reach your turnoff at the exact mile don't worry — it should be just around the corner! Most of the trailheads lie at the end of dirt roads. And dirt roads vary in quality. You may be early and lucky, driving over a wet spot a few days before it becomes a bottomless mudhole. You may be lucky and late, following the road's annual grading by a day or two. Or, you may be unlucky. But normally, most of these roads can be driven by passenger cars. Be sure to carry a shovel and bucket when you drive forest roads. They are required during times of high fire danger.

Idaho's roads are among America's most dangerous. These dangers are increased by the discourteous drivers who seem to abound on dirt roads. There are several rules of law and courtesy you should follow when driving the back roads. When two vehicles meet on a one lane road, the one headed downhill must back up until a suitable turnout is reached. Drivers should adjust their speed so they can stop in one half the distance they can see ahead. On weekdays, you must use extra caution because of logging trucks. When someone appears on your tail, slow down and pull over or stop, so they can safely pass. Slow down to a crawl when you pass pedestrians or horsemen on the road, so you don't coat them with dust. And watch for animals, since 500 auto-animal collisions occur in Idaho each year. AND-good luck!

The maps that accompany the trail descriptions are drawn at a scale of one half inch to the mile. Contours are shown with 500 foot intervals. The trailhead and day, overnight, and weekend hiking goals are depicted by "T", "D", "O", and "W".

Sources

Addresses

Idaho Panhandle N.F.
Box 310
Coeur d'Alene, ID 83814

Clearwater N.F.
Route 4
Orofino, ID 83544

Nez Perce N.F.
319 E. Main
Grangeville, ID 83530

Hells Canyon National Recreation Area
Idaho Office
3620 B Snake River Road
Lewiston, ID 83501

Bitterroot N.F.
316 N. 3rd
Hamilton, MT 59840

Kootenai N.F.
Box AS
Libby, MT 59923

Colville N.F.
Colville, WA

Bureau of Land Management
Coeur d'Alene District Office
Box 1889
Coeur d'Alene, ID 83814

U.S Geological Survey
Branch of Distribution
Federal Center
Denver, CO 80225

Idaho Department of Fish & Game
Box 25
Boise, ID 83707

Idaho Bureau of Mines & Geology
University of Idaho
Moscow, ID 83843

Idaho Bureau of Tourism
Room 108, Capitol Building
Boise, ID 83720

Idaho Outfitters and Guides Association
Box 95
Boise, ID 83701

Books

Alt and Hyndman. *Roadside Geology of the Northern Rockies.* Missoula, MT: Mountain Press, 1972.

Ross and Savage. *Idaho Earth Science.* Moscow, ID: Idaho Bureau of Mines and Geology, 1967.

Reid, Bittner, et al. *Geologic Section and Road Log Across the Idaho Batholith.* Moscow, ID: Idaho Bureau of Mines and Geology, 1979.

Larrison, Earl. *Birds of the Pacific Northwest.* Moscow: University Press of Idaho, 1981.

Larrison and Johnson. *Mammals of Idaho.* Moscow: University Press of Idaho, 1981.

Hart, John. *Walking Softly in the Wilderness: The Sierra Club Guide to Backpacking.* San Francisco: Sierra Club Books, 1977.

Manning, Harvey. *Backpacking: One Step at a Time.* New York: Vintage, 1972.

Rethmel, R.C. *Backpacking.* Minneapolis, MN: Burgess Publishing Co., 1968.

Bluestein, S.R. *Hiking Trails of Southern Idaho.* Caldwell, Idaho: Caxton Printers, 1981.

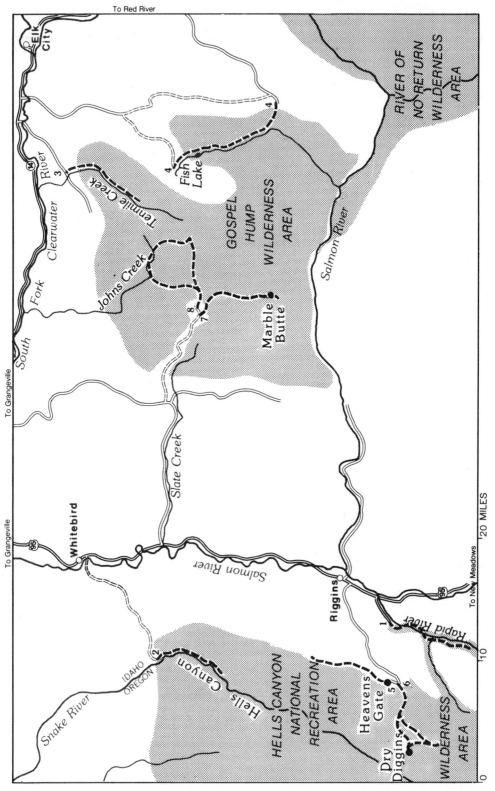

To Red River

ELK City

River Clearwater

South Fork

To Grangeville

To Grangeville

Whitebird

95

Snake River

IDAHO
OREGON

Hells Canyon

HELLS CANYON NATIONAL RECREATION AREA

Heavens Gate

Dry Diggins

WILDERNESS AREA

Salmon River

Slate Creek

Riggins

Rapid River

To New Meadows

95

Tenmile Creek

Johns Creek

Fish Lake

GOSPEL HUMP WILDERNESS AREA

Marble Butte

Salmon River

RIVER OF NO RETURN WILDERNESS AREA

3

4

4

8
7

2

1

5
6

20 MILES

10

0

Hells Canyon and the Gospel Hump

Spectacular Hells Canyon is America's deepest gorge. He Devil, 9393 feet high, is only five miles from the Snake River, 1300 feet low. While Southern Idaho's main transportation routes follow the Snake, and North Idaho is linked to the Pacific by Snake River dams and locks, the Hells Canyon stretch of river has long been a barrier to communication and transportation. Even today, there is neither a complete trail system nor any foot bridges that cross the river. This wild stretch of river has had a controversial past, and only with the establishment of the Hells Canyon National Recreation Area (HCNRA) have dams been banned from the gorge.

One of the most exciting features of the HCNRA is the mountains it includes. While the Grand Canyon of the Colorado is bordered by the Kaibab, which means "mountain lying down," the Grand Canyon of the Snake is bordered by the Seven Devils, mountains which certainly do stand up. The Seven Devils have had as controversial a past as Hells Canyon. Severely overgrazed in the early 1900's, they became a favorite haunt of trail bikers, who generally used the area responsibly and improved parts of the trail system. Geologists also frequented these mountains, investigating their copper and silver potential. All these people were excluded by the HCNRA Act of 1975, which halted mineral entry in the entire NRA and banned motorcycles from the Hells Canyon Wilderness Area.

The Seven Devils Mountains are included in that Wilderness. They are a compact range (the whole Hells Canyon Wilderness Area is only 194,000 acres, and much of this is oversteepened canyon slopes.) The Devils are divided into northern and southern portions by Horse Heaven Lookout. The northern half is ringed by a 28 mile loop trail. This trail accesses steep creeks up which trails climb or routes scramble to mountain lakes. The loop trail reflects the dryness of the mountain range as a whole, and has a long dry stretch from Baldy Lake Creek to Dog Creek. The scarcity of good water sources in the area means you can't be as choosy as you might like about water, so you should definitely carry or use some purification device or method.

The HCNRA has published a series of pamphlets on natural history and recreational opportunities. It has information centers in Lewiston and Riggins.

The Gospel Hump is Idaho's least known Wilderness Area. It was born in a compromise worked out between conservationists eager to preserve the area's fragile soils and abundant wildlife, and timber and mineral advocates who sought to ensure continuing access to the area's natural resources. A 206,000 acre wilderness was established, while large roadless areas along the South Fork Clearwater River and on Little Slate Creek were scheduled for development. This compromise short-circuited the USFS planning process. It resulted in a wilderness area with such contorted boundaries that management as wilderness is nearly impossible. Repeated incursions by motor vehicles have been made into the wilderness. Some have been ignored by the Forest Service where wilderness boundaries were poorly drawn. The Nez Perce, short on trail funds like all other National Forests, has been unable to afford the major trail reconstruction so critically needed throughout the Gospel Hump area. Trails in this area seem to be of just two types: too level to erode, or badly eroded and getting worse. Literally hundreds of water bars and many miles of trail relocation are needed.

That's all the bad news—now for the good. A hike in the Gospel Hump can be a very rewarding experience. The breaks area to the south of the Hump Trail is well suited to cross-country travel, while the valleys of upper Johns and Twentymile Creeks are ideal for trailless exploration. The outstanding scenery and great opportunities for solitude do make this a prime backpacking area. Moose and elk abound, and your chances for sighting game are excellent. Idahoans need to visit the Gospel Hump area to experience its natural beauties and ponder its future.

1. Rapid River

Hikes: D, O, W, E.
Total Distance, W: 16 miles.
Difficulty: Level II.
Season: March 1—September 20.
Elevation Gain: 1800 feet.
USGS Maps: Pollock Mountain,
  Heavens Gate.
USFS Map: Nez Perce N.F.
Mileage, Lew: 114½ (3 dirt).

Introduction: The Rapid River is one of Idaho's jewels, and it drains a roadless area supremely deserving of affection and protection. The river and its West Fork have been named Wild Rivers and appended to the HCNRA, making a wishbone-shaped addition. The Rapid River is trailed for 24 of its 27 miles, and offers an exciting catalogue of central Idaho wilderness, from streamside desert at the trailhead (2200 feet) to high coniferous forest at its source (7500 feet). The trail is rated Level II because of its rocky stretches and shortage of good campsites for the first 8 miles.

The Trail: Weekenders will want to reach at least Wyant Camp, 8 miles in. Dayhikers can stop anywhere as far as the West Fork confluence (4 miles in), while overnighters will need to go past that mark to reach the first sizeable camping area (4½ miles). While the trailhead is signed, the first stretch of trail is hard to follow. Just climb on the road and take a trail whenever you can. Soon you'll enter the Rapid River narrows, where a limestone formation has provided many nesting cavities for birds. Cross the river on the first of many new bridges, replacements for those washed out by a great flood in the early 1970's. (The lesson of that catastrophe seems to have been lost on homeowners in the subdivision downstream.) You now hike above the river and get a view of grassy slopes on the other side, where deer and bear forage. The second crossing is followed by an exciting point where the river has undercut the rock on which the trail runs.

A climb brings you to the signed junction with the West Fork Trail, where you bear left for the main river. There is a campsite up the West Fork from the bridge, but the best camps are just up the main river. They are too close to the water and the trail to meet the highest standards, but they are the best ones on the trail's first 6 miles. Past Cora Gulch you begin a climb that takes you away from the riverside grand fir and up to the high benches' magnificent mix of open forest and grassy meadows. The semi-level areas before Dutch Oven Creek invite you to camp in this splendid environment. Past the creek you climb beside some truly ponderous yellow pines and bear left to a signed trail divide. Go left again, unless you wish to challenge this Bryan Mountain Trail which climbs hard and high and dry. At last you descend a beautiful meadow to reach Wyant Creek, where you turn left and go down to Wyant Camp, a grassy opening above Rapid River. There is more good camping on benches and bars before the next bridge.

Extensions: Your best bet is to explore the forgotten land between the main river and its West Fork. All the trails shown on your USGS map are signed, with the Copper Creek Trail looking superior. There is also a trail leaving the Black Lake Fork area that goes to Twin Lakes. Upstream from Wyant Camp, campsites become more numerous, with the Copper Creek and Paradise Cabin areas most suitable.

Access: Drive south from Spalding Junction 111 miles on US-95, to the Rapid River Road, 3½ miles south of Riggins. Turn right and drive 3 miles to the end of the road. The trail is not the road along the river, but rather the road just a few feet to its right. There is no nearby USFS campground; the hatchery area is closed to camping; the hills beyond the gates are not conducive to camping; and there are very few campable spots on the trail's first four miles. The commercial campground on Squaw Creek near Riggins is an alternative. The HCNRA has long range plans to improve this trailhead.

Paradise Cabin

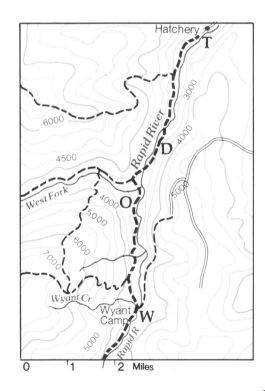

2. Hells Canyon

Hikes: D, O, W, E.
Total Distance, W: 17 miles.
Difficulty: Level II.
Season: March 1 — September 20.
Elevation Gain: 900 feet.
USGS Maps: Kirkwood Creek,
   Kernan Point (1:62,500).
USFS Map: Nez Perce N.F.
Mileage, Lew: 101 (18 dirt).

Introduction: The Snake River Trail in Hells Canyon offers some of Idaho's finest springtime hiking. Pittsburg Landing is the main access point, since it is hard to reach the canyon from the south. Two trails, one on each side, begin within ten miles of Hells Canyon Dam, but you must have a boat to reach them. The Idaho side trail continues 30 miles north to Pittsburg Landing, while the Oregon side trail goes all the way to Dug Bar, about 50 miles north. Suspension bridges or cable cars would allow hikers to easily loop the canyon, but at present you have only three ways to cross the river: carry your own raft (risky), flag down a jet boat (unlikely in spring when hiking is best), or make arrangements with a commercial operator (contact through HCNRA). The trail south of Pittsburg is Level II due to some steep, rocky stretches. Springtime in Hells Canyon is also grazing time, so be sure to boil all your water. Carry a stove to do this: there is very little firewood in the canyon.

The Trail: There are many campsites for overnight and weekend hikers between the trailhead and Caribou Creek, 11 miles in. Lower Kirby Rapids, 3 miles in, would make a good dayhiker's goal. The trail is easy to follow as it leaves Klopton Creek. The first campsites are below and above China Rapids. You must make a steep climb up Line Gulch, a refreshingly cool, green change from the rocky, exposed trail. There are many more campsites near Lower Kirby Rapids. The Kirby Creek bar below the trail is private land.

You continue to climb from Kirby Creek, and at last descend a poor stretch of trail to Kirkwood Bar, the "Home below Hells Canyon" where former Senator Len Jordan once lived. At the bottom of a rough road which is usually impassable in spring, it is being developed to interpret the ranching history of Hells Canyon. You can camp at the downstream end of the bar. A half-mile past Kirkwood you come to Halfmoon Bar, where there is camping. From there you climb to Suicide Point (above Big Bar on your USGS map). From its splendid viewpoint you can see many campsites on the benches and bars from there to Caribou Creek.

Extensions: Sheep Creek is 8 miles, Granite Creek 19 miles from Suicide Point. Trails lead up both creeks to the Seven Devils high country.

Access: Drive 80 miles south of Spalding Junction to Whitebird Bridge. Continue 1½ miles south and turn right. After 1½ miles turn left, cross the old Salmon River bridge, and turn left again. After 7¼ more miles, bear right on the Deer Creek Road for Pittsburg Saddle. An additional 2¾ miles brings you to another right turn. The road deteriorates from here, and its steep grades can be hazardous when wet. When you reach the flats after about 5½ miles of descent, go left and drive right through a gate at a ranch (leave the gate as you find it!). Another 1½ miles bring you to the trailhead, where there is some camping. On the trail, campsites begin in one mile. The HCNRA plans to upgrade the road to and build a campground at Pittsburg Landing — a much needed improvement for this vital access point.

Suicide Point view

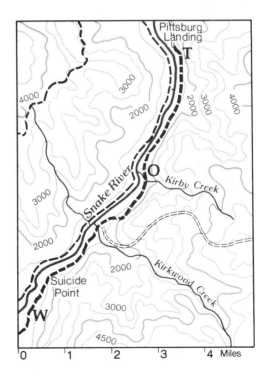

3. Tenmile Creek

Hikes: D, O, W.
Total Distance, W: 12 miles.
Difficulty: Level II.
Season: June 15 — September 20.
Elevation Gain: 1600 feet.
USGS Maps: North Pole, Golden*.
USFS Map: Nez Perce N.F.
Mileage: 114½ (12 dirt).

Introduction: Tenmile Creek drains the north slope of Beargrass Ridge. The trail that ascends it makes for good hiking, and offers exciting possibilities for extended loops. This is one of the easiest-to-reach trails in the Gospel Hump Wilderness. Access is via the Santiam-Sourdough Road, newly improved to help the USFS harvest timber in areas released by the Gospel Hump compromise. The trail does a funny thing: it gets better as it goes along. But the boggy, rocky stretch at the start rates it as Level II. This area is grazed, so treat your water.

The Trail: Weekenders will want to reach the large camping area near Tenmile Meadows, 6 miles in. Overnighters and day hikers may stop near the Williams Creek Ridge or the Driveway Extension Trails, 3 miles in. The trailhead is well marked and the trail easy to follow as it moves through bogs and over rocks. This would be a good gaiter hike in June and early July. The two trail junctions are located where shown on your USGS map, and they are signed. There are campsites just past both junctions, with a few more past the intermittent stream at 4600 feet. Beyond the second junction, the trail forsakes the rugged stream bottom for the gentle slopes above, and the hiking becomes much easier. Good camping begins when you near the "Campsite" shown on your map. The trail here differs from the map: the Tenmile Creek Trail crosses a side creek, climbs to the left, and *then* meets the North Pole Trail, which does not directly connect with the "Campsite". When you cross the side creek you enter a level lodgepole forest. Side paths access campsites near the memorable creek. The main trail avoids Tenmile Creek for a while longer, passing campsites until it meets the creek across from Tenmile Meadows. There are more campsites one mile farther down the trail.

Extensions: Many loops are possible off this trail. One would cut west to Twentymile Creek and Lake, then go south to Beargrass Ridge and Squaw Meadows. Another would cut east to North Pole and return via Squaw Meadows.

Access: Drive south from Spalding Junction to ID-13, Grangeville Junction, and turn left. Drive 1¼ miles through the town to the Mt. Idaho Road. Turn right, and after ¾ more miles turn left. Descend to the South Fork Clearwater River, and 27 miles past your junction with the river road turn right on the new Sourdough-Santiam Road. The trailhead is 12 miles up the road. You can camp to the north of the trailhead, or in level areas in the first ½ mile of trail.

Tenmile Meadows

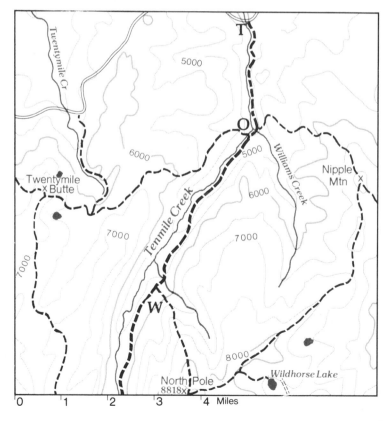

19

4. Fish Lake

Hikes: D, W, E.
Total Distance, W: 22 miles.
Difficulty: Level II.
Season: June 15 – September 15.
Elevation Gain: 2200 feet.
USGS Map: Silver Spur Ridge.
USFS Maps: Red River Ranger District
   (Nez Perce N.F.); or, Nez Perce N.F.
Mileage, Lew: 147¼ (5½ dirt)

Introduction: The Gospel Hump Wilderness Area has two major exclusions, the Moores Station Road to the west and the Hump Mining District to the east. Isolated by this mining district is the drainage of Lake Creek, a tributary to the same Crooked Creek that flows through Dixie town. Access to this area is from either Halfway Campground near Dixie Guard Station or from the Mining District, reached via a rough road from Orogrande. The Crooked Creek Trail near Halfway House passes through spectacularly contorted high-grade metamorphic rocks. Its rocky nature makes it a Level II hike. The trail from the mining road is less rocky: Level I.

The Trails: From Halfway, weekenders will hike 11 miles to Fish Lake (or better, set up a camp before the lake and dayhike on to it). Overnighters would have to hike 6½ miles to reach a campsite on Silver Spur Creek. The bridge at Lake Creek, 3 miles in, makes a good dayhiker's goal. The trail starts just above the campground. It passes through a beautiful gorge and crosses a good bridge over Big Creek (treat its water before you drink it) on its way to Lake Creek. Take a right turn at the Lake Creek Bridge and begin to climb on the rocky trail. Above Jim Sandy Creek the trail changes from rock to soil, but the first good campsites don't come until Silver Spur Creek. The best camping is in the lodgepole flats that start near the Jumbo Canyon Trail junction. From here to Fish Lake you have a richly deserved cakewalk. The lake is an excellent place to watch for moose.

From the mining road, the lake is a two mile hike. Descend on the occasionally boggy trail. At one spot you come close to the beautiful, meandering creek. A brief rocky descent brings you to lake level and campsites.

Extensions: You can descend Crooked Creek to the Salmon River. You could also climb from Crooked Creek to Oregon Butte, a desolate and scenic lookout, and then return via Jumbo Canyon. Trail No. 229, which is supposed to descend Silver Spur Ridge and tie in with the Lake Creek Trail, was not visible.

Access: Drive south from Spalding Junction on US-95 to Grangeville. Turn left on ID-13 and drive 1¼ miles through town. Turn right and then left after ¾ mile. Go through Mt. Idaho and down to the South Fork Clearwater River. After 32 miles you come to the Crooked River Road. Turn right for Orogrande and the mining road access point. Follow signs for the Buffalo Hump and Orogrande Summit, bearing right when you pass Orogrande. The Hump Road is steep but generally passable for sedans. At the top of the hill bear left. The descent to the trailhead is a nasty four-wheel-drive road. Since the trailhead is only 1¾ miles down it, you could easily park here and walk the distance. There is a USFS campground at Orogrande Summit.

For the Halfway House trailhead, continue up the South Fork Clearwater Road to Elk City Junction, 4 miles past Crooked River. Turn right on Red River Road, and follow the paved road through Dixie town to Dixie Guard Station junction, 5½ miles farther. Take a left there, and then a right to reach Halfway House Campground, which has just four units. There are other campsites along the road back to Dixie. No campsites on this trail for 6 miles.

A face only a mother could love

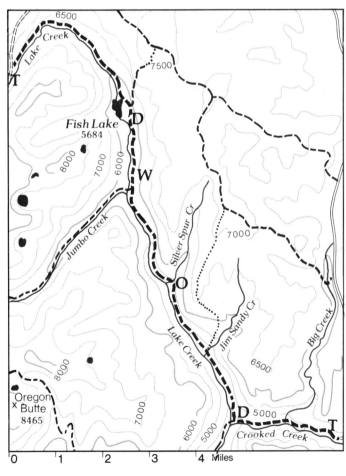

5. North of Heavens Gate

Hikes: D, O, W.
Total Distance, O: 8 miles.
Difficulty: Level II.
Season: July 1 – September 15.
Elevation Gain: 1050 feet.
USGS Maps: Kessler Creek,
  Heavens Gate.
USFS Map: Nez Perce N.F.
Mileage, Lew: 127 (17 dirt).

Introduction: The original Hells Canyon-Seven Devils Scenic Area, precursor to the Hells Canyon Wilderness Area, did not include the lower Sheep Creek drainage or the Cold Springs-Heavens Gate ridge to the east. Now, the wilderness boundary is formed by the trail that follows this ridge, and a curious trail and boundary they are. About two-thirds of the trail is an old road bulldozed out as a fire break. And some important wildlife and human habitat areas east of the trail were not included in the wilderness (though motorized access to them seems unlikely). Nevertheless, this trail offers good hiking, camping, and sightseeing. While it is not too difficult, Level II hiking skills are needed to cope with the lack of water.

The Trail: The overnighter's and dayhiker's goal is The Narrows, 4 miles in. Weekenders can camp there and dayhike on to Crater Lake, about 3 miles further. Start by descending some ill-defined switchbacks from the Heaven's Gate parking lot. Once at the saddle, take the rightmost trail and climb along the east flank of the ridge, an area blessed with a magnificent stand of whitebark pine. There is no blazed route to the campsites by Papoose Lake. You can reach the lake by cutting off the trail to the right when it starts to level off after climbing 8210. Contour and descend until you see the gully due south of the lake. This drainage, the direct route, is very steep, and you might choose to detour down the ridge.

As your USGS map shows, beyond 8210 the trail switches to the west side of the ridge. And where the red tick mark appears near the top of Section 29, the pack trail becomes a jeep trail. At the signed Squaw Creek Trail junction above The Narrows, this jeep road becomes a sedan road – a strange experience for wilderness. The Narrows area is a minicirque of great beauty. The snow that it holds until late July can be melted for water (a technique better known to winter campers), and this meagre source is the only one available for the rest of the hike. There are good campsites along the road and in the adjacent drainage (shown on your USGS map with an intermittent stream).

If you continue north from The Narrows, you will climb to Fire Camp Saddle. Just before it comes the signed Indian Springs Trail junction and a stunning view down Sheep Creek to the Snake River (6200 feet below). You may notice a well-blazed trail descending to the right of the saddle just before 7176. Don't take it for a short cut to Crater Lake, or you will have the joyous experience of blundering along brushy game trails and wandering aimlessly in the Grave Creek drainage. The true route to Crater Lake comes after the steep descent from 7176, past the signed Lightning Ridge Trail junction. It is merely a blazed path that descends to the lake, which usually runs dry in September. Until then, its unappetizing waters attract much game, and a campsite near it would be creaky and creepy with the sounds of passing elk and deer and the tastes of stagnant water.

Extensions: The wildest part of the Hells Canyon Wilderness lies to the west of this trail, in lower Sheep Creek. You could dscend the Squaw Creek or Lightning Ridge Trails and return to Windy Saddle via the East Fork Sheep Creek Trail or the Dry Diggins Trail (which is aptly named for its lack of water).

Access: Same as Dry Diggins (page 24), except that at Windy Saddle you turn right and drive to Heaven's Gate Lookout parking lot. You can camp at the Seven Devils Campground, or hike 1½ miles to a Papoose Lake campsite, or make a dry camp on 8210.

Open country north of Heavens Gate

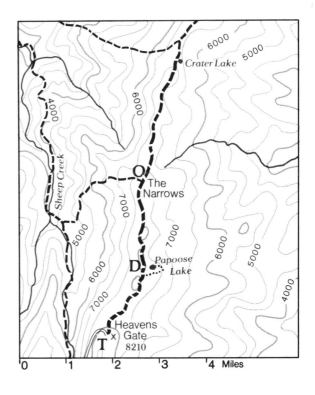

6. Dry Diggins

Hikes: D, W, E.
Total Distance, W: 20 miles.
Difficulty: Level II.
Season: July 1—September 15.
Elevation Gain: 4100 feet.
USGS Map: He Devil (1:62,500).
USFS Map: Nez Perce N.F.
Mileage, Lew: 127 (17 dirt).

Introduction: The Seven Devils are at their best in this hike. You not only have views of the heights, especially the magnificent and challenging pass between He Devil and She Devil, but also of the depths, most notably the 6700 foot drop from Dry Diggins Lookout to the Snake River. This is a rocky, rough trail that will challenge Level II hikers.

The Trail: A good loop would go to Bernard Lakes, 8 miles in, and then return via Dry Diggins and Hibbs Cow Camp, some 20 miles in all. Dayhikers can hike 2 miles to the view of He Devil and Sheep Creek below 8255. Begin by taking the trail that starts northnortheast of the outhouse at Windy Saddle. Don't go down the dry, gravelly wash. After a few switchbacks' descent, you contour across the head of East Fork Sheep Creek, where there is water. A climb then takes you to a good view of He Devil and the descent to the West Fork Sheep Creek, which dayhikers needn't worry about.

There are a very few campsites at the crossing of Sheep Creek. From there you cross another branch of the creek and then climb on a new trail, which bears to the right of the old one your USGS map shows. A healthy climb brings you to a main trail junction where you must make a choice. Straight ahead lie Bernard Lakes, which have few campsites and poor water; Dry Diggins Lookout is just above the lakes. To the left is Hibbs Cow Camp, which offers excellent water and good dispersed campsites. A trail leads to the lookout from there, too.

If you go straight, to the lakes, you make a very rough and rocky descent to the clear waters of Bernard Creek. Here are the best campsites and waters on this trail.

There are campsites at the next three Bernard Lakes. A trail leaves the last lake's outlet, climbs to the left, and then cuts right to reach the saddle below the lookout. You can dayhike up for the view, return for your pack, and then hike southeast on the trail that passes 8099. There are many dry campsites on this delightful trail. The junction with your return trail is at a big bare area (a legacy of overgrazing?). After a short hike south of here, you encounter the Granite Creek Trail, which quickly takes you to the excellent springs and spacious camping at the old Cow Camp.

If you reach the main junction and decide to go to Hibbs Cow Camp, turn left and follow the level Granite Creek Trail, bearing right when it meets the Sheep Lakes Trail and left when it meets the Dry Diggins Lookout Trail.

Extensions: You could continue south on the Potato Hill Trail to Horse Heaven and return to Windy Saddle via the Boise Trail. The nine mile stretch from Baldy Lake Creek to Dog Creek is dry. Or, you could just explore the west side lakes: Echo, Baldy, and Triangle.

Access: Drive 108 miles south on US-95 from Spalding Junction, to Riggins. Then drive one mile past town to the Squaw Creek Road, where you turn right. After 1½ miles on this steep road bear left. The crucial turnoff comes 9½ miles from the highway, when the Seven Devils Road turns right and climbs. After 6¾ more miles you come to Windy Saddle, where there is a trailhead parking area. The Seven Devils Campground is just down the road to the left of Windy Saddle. The first campsites along the trail are a long 4 miles in, at West Fork Sheep Creek.

24

Residents of the Seven Devils

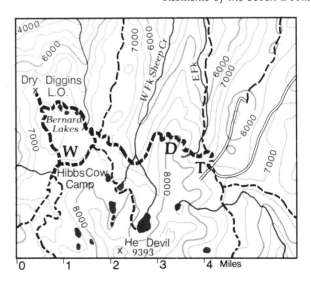

7. Marble Butte

Hikes: D, O, W, E.
Total Distance, W: 18 miles.
Difficulty: Level I.
Season: July 10 — September 15.
Elevation Gain: 2900 feet.
USGS Maps: Hanover Mountain*,
   Marble Butte.
USFS Map: Nez Perce N.F.
Mileage, Lew: 109¼ miles (30 dirt).

Introduction: Hiking differs greatly depending on whether you are north or south of the Square Mountain Road. To the north, trails drop off steeply to meet John's Creek, often passing lakes along the way. To the south, they tend to follow ridges that reluctantly, and then steeply, drop off into the depths of the Salmon River Gorge. These southern trails offer cool springs, emerald meadows, and views of endless sunsets. This one is generally easy to follow and not too rocky — Level I.

The Trail: Overnighters may camp in Anchor Meadows, 3 miles in; dayhikers will want to go on to a view from Sheep Mountain, 4 miles; while weekenders can camp in meadows below Plummer Peak (6 miles) or by a stream at North Butte (9 miles). Start by following the old Hump Road for 3 miles to Anchor Meadows. This road, severely eroded by the wagons, packstock, and feet of miners, crosses a tributary of Anchor Creek and then bears left to reach the meadows. This portion of trail has not been included in the wilderness. When you come to the trail junction at the far side of the meadows, turn south on the Black Butte Lookout Trail. Cross the creek and enter the Gospel Hump Wilderness Area. Climb to a meadow on the flank of Sheep Mountain where you have a view of the ridges ahead. Descend to a wet saddle, and then climb again to Plummer Point. There are dry

campsites on the ridge here, and wet sites in the meadows below. These meadows were carved by glaciers that at one time may have formed an ice cap over all the Gospel Hump high country.

Continuing on, you descend to the saddle just east of Ace Creek. Despite indications to the contrary on your USGS map, Ace Creek does not flow close to the saddle. Good water *is* available from several springs on the east side of Marble Butte, and from an unnamed stream the trail passes after its descent from Marble Butte (just north of North Butte). You can camp in Porcupine Meadows or near that unnamed creek.

Access: Drive 65 miles south from Spalding Junction on US-95 to Grangeville, where you turn left. Drive 1¼ miles through town to the Grangeville-Salmon Road, where you turn right. When you come to the road junction after ¾ mile, go straight. Follow this main road for 29¾ miles, to the Square Mountain Road. Turn left on this very rough and very steep road. Only the gutsiest passenger cars should proceed past the West Fork Gospel Creek trailhead, 4 miles up; four wheel drive would certainly be necessary in wet weather. Follow the road 12 miles to Moores Station, a USFS guard station with good water. This is your trailhead. You can camp along the road, or 3 miles down the trail in Anchor Meadows.

Looking across Sheep Creek to Oregon Butte

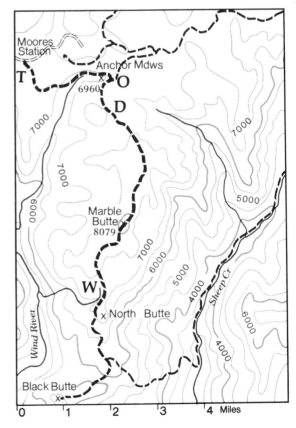

8. Upper Johns Creek

Hikes: D, O, W, E.
Total Distance, W: 24 miles.
Difficulty: Levels II, III.
Season: July 10 — September 15.
Elevation Gain: 4100 feet.
USGS Maps: Sourdough Peak,
   Marble Butte.
USFS Map: Nez Perce N.F.
Mileage, Lew: 110¼ (31 dirt).

Introduction: This loop hike is a difficult but rewarding trip that introduces you to the full range of Gospel Hump environments. Along the way you can see moose swimming in mountain lakes, a trail rich in history, elk browsing with their young, and a beautiful creek in transition from meanders in meadows to cascades in canyons. The hike is Level II down to Twin Lakes and along Beargrass Ridge, and Level III on the steep trails that descend to Johns Creek.

The Trail: Dayhikers can walk the Hump Trail along Beargrass Ridge as far as they want, or cut off it to Square Mountain Lake. Overnighters can reach Twin Lakes (4 miles) or one of many camps on Beargrass Ridge (3-5 miles). Hardy weekenders can do the 24 mile loop via Johns Creek (which makes a better three day than two day loop). You start by skirting meadows and crossing a stream along the south flank of Square Mountain. Turn left on the signed Twin Lakes Trail. The trail your USFS map shows going east to Upper Twin Lake from 7752 is in very poor condition, so go down the main trail to the signed Twin Lakes turnoff. There are campsites at the inlet end of Lower Twin Lake, and a good spring just southwest of the camping area. A route to Upper Twin Lake (known for its Pacific Giant Salamanders) passes the spring, climbs to the right, and sidehills to the lake, where you can camp. When the trail that descends to John's Creek is flat, it is in good condition; but when it slopes, it is badly eroded. After you have passed the Cross Trail and turned left at the Kentucky Creek Trail junction, you meet the Straight-Down-to-John's-Creek Trail. Take it to the creek, where you can camp. This area is the

heart of the Gospel Hump Wilderness Area, visited by few. Cross the creek, climb to a bench, turn right, and you soon pass two sheepherder huts. Campsites follow, and then comes an unsigned junction. To the left is the John's Creek Trail, to the right the Kentucky Creek cutoff trail. Go left on this peaceful, open trail with campsites. When at last it is time to cross Johns Creek, ignore your USGS map and cross *beyond* the two intermittent streams it shows. The trail is well blazed here and the crossing is obvious. Fill your canteens when you reach Taylor Creek Meadows and campsites, and skirt the meadows' western edge.

Take the trail that comes after the Boundary Creek Stock Driveway and climbs to the right, up the ridge. This joins the Kentucky Creek Trail for the climb to Beargrass Ridge, a climb that starts gently and ends harshly. There is a consolation, however, in your overviews of Taylor Creek's ultra-steep headlands. The spring shown on your map at 6800 feet is unreliable; however, there are good springs starting right at the top of the Marble Butte quadrangle. You may camp near these or near the headwaters of Hagen Creek next to the Beargrass Ridge Trail. That trail is the old Hump Road, and "old" is one of the nicest things one can say about it. It is quite rocky and it eschews such conveniences as contouring, instead going from summit to summit. Frequent streams make finding an off-the-beaten-track campsite in the forests and meadows of this broad ridge an easy task. The trail that returns you to your Square Mountain trailhead veers off to the right of the old road, and it is signed.

Extensions: From Johns Creek you could explore the Taylor and Boundary Creek meadows and headlands. Or, you could continue east along Beargrass Ridge to Squaw Meadows or Hidden Lake.

Access: Follow directions for Marble Butte, page 26, but drive a mile past Moores Station to the signed trailhead. You might camp beside the stream ½ mile in, or along the road, or on top of Square Mountain.

Taylor Creek headlands

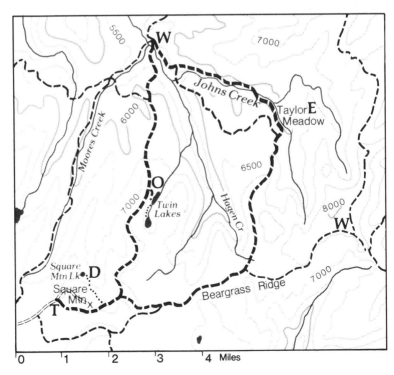

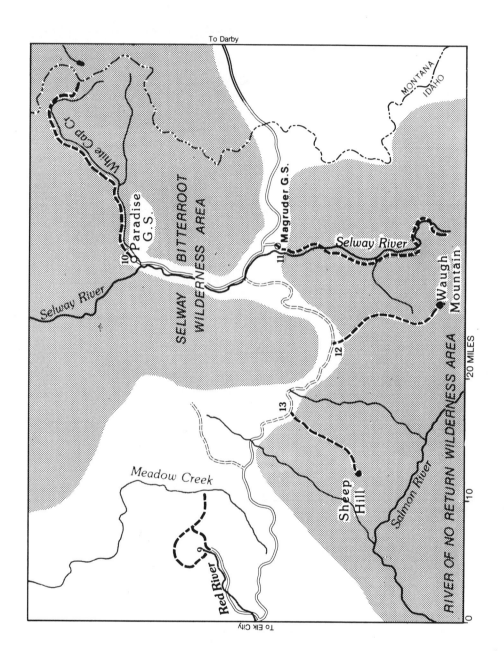

The Magruder Corridor

There is no wilderness in the world like that formed by the River of No Return and Selway Bitterroot Wilderness Areas. Totalling over four million acres, the two are only separated by a dirt road, and even this road is named after a trail: the Nez Perce Trail Road. This was the main Nez Perce Indian route to the buffalo grounds of western Montana and eastern Idaho; had Lewis and Clark's guide found it, they would have been spared their ordeal on the Lolo Trail, a much inferior route for crossing the Central Idaho wilderness. Samuel Parker, the missionary who recruited the ill-fated Whitmans, travelled this route in 1835 and shaved some two weeks of Lewis and Clark's time. The Road was only opened in 1936. Portions were improved in the 1960's when the Forest Service planned to log the area. Citizen opposition forced a reevaluation of this plan, and the River of No Return Wilderness Act laid the issue of logging or wilderness to rest in 1980, when much of the land adjoining the road became wilderness. Unfortunately, what's not wilderness *will* be logged, and the Trail Road's western 15 miles will soon see logging traffic.

Since Magruder Guard Station is the only inhabited point on the Nez Perce Trail Road from Red River to Montana, this narrow strip of non-wilderness is known as the Magruder Corridor. Many trails head south from this road into the Salmon River Breaks. That area is characterized by high, dry ridges and soaring peaks that conceal mountain lakes and offer vistas far to the south across the Salmon River Gorge. Other trails head north into the little-used southern part of the Selway Bitterroot Wilderness. They are dominated less by ridges than by streams such as the Selway and Little Clearwater Rivers, and Running, White Cap, and Bargamin Creeks. This road does not open up until mid- to late July, and it is essential that you check with the Nez Perce or Bitterroot National Forests before trying to traverse it. There is really only one bad stretch of the road, from Dry Saddle to Salmon Mountain, and it shouldn't cause problems for any but the most low-riding cars. At any rate, you won't want to hurry on the Nez Perce Trail Road. The scenery is just too stunning to race through.

9. Red River Loop

Hikes: D, O, W, E.
Total Distance, W: 17 miles.
Difficulty: Level I.
Season: June 15 — September 15.
Elevation Gain: 2300 feet.
USGS Map: Sable Hill.
USFS Map: Nez Perce N.F.
Mileage, Lew: 136 (9½ dirt).

Introduction: The upper Red River was once as beautiful a stream as Meadow Creek is today. Now it is an environmental disaster area. Huge clearcuts have resisted repeated attempts to plant trees. With every storm they pour precious soil into the river, which runs as muddy as the Mississippi. Trails from Red River access Meadow Creek, which will hopefully be treated more gently. A good loop hike is possible in this popular area, a part of which is closed to trail bikes. This is easy Level I hiking once you find the trails and figure out their junctions.

The Trail: A 13 mile loop hike goes up the Otterson Creek Trail to Red River Ridge, southeast to the source of Red River, and then southwest to the Hot Spring area along the river. An additional four mile round trip would take you to Meadow Creek. Dayhikers could hike up the Otterson Creek or Red River Trails, and overnighters can find camps along Butter Creek, 4½ miles in on the Red River Trail. Fill your canteens and then start the loop by finding the Otterson Creek Trail. Begin at the trailhead sign on an old road that cuts left just beyond the Shissler Creek/Red River bridge. This road leads to a bridge across Bridge Creek, and then joins the "Jeep Trail" your USGS map shows. Turn left on it, and the Otterson Creek Trail is the eroded rut you see climbing behind the "Closed to Motor Vehicles" sign. Ascending the trail, which improves in quality, you pass possible campsites on the ridge at about 5400 feet, just 200 feet above a fork of Otterson Creek. (A very old trail appears and reappears along stretches of this creek, whose waters are very sweet.) The junction with the ridge trail comes at a big meadow.

Turn right and follow the ridge. After the trail drops off the ridge and contours along the mountain's right flank, watch for an unsigned but easy-to-spot trail junction. Cut left there and climb a short way to another trail junction. Turn right here and descend until you can hear the good waters of Butter Creek. You can camp along the creek where it runs close to the trail, at about 6000 feet. The Meadow Creek-Red River trail junction has changed since your USGS map was published. The river trail now meets the ridge and Meadow Creek trails in the same place, making a four-way intersection which is well signed. The Meadow Creek Trail descends to the left, crosses Butter Creek, climbs and then descends to a vast meadow. There are many campsites along the way and at Meadow Creek. The Red River Trail back to the Hot Springs is easy to follow, with a few steep spots as it crosses its numerous side creeks. Trees screen the trail from the pathetic clearcuts on the other side of the creek. When you come out on a poor road you are only a few yards from the good road. The Otterson Creek trailhead is ¾ mile from here.

Extensions: You could turn left on the Red River Ridge Trail and take a right on the trail that descends to Meadow Creek Guard Station, and then return by way of Sable Hill. Or, you could explore upper Meadow Creek before it's all logged.

Access: Follow directions for Sheep Hill as far as Red River Ranger Station. Turn left on the Hot Springs road, and after 9½ miles, just past a bridge, watch on your left for the Otterson Creek Trail sign. The first campsites on the Otterson Creek Trail come when it levels off about 2 miles in. To reach the Red River Trail, drive to the junction ¼ mile past the Otterson Creek Trail, turn right, and drive another ½ mile. The USFS discourages roadside camping along Red River because of sanitation problems, so please use a campground.

Meadow Creek, 1980

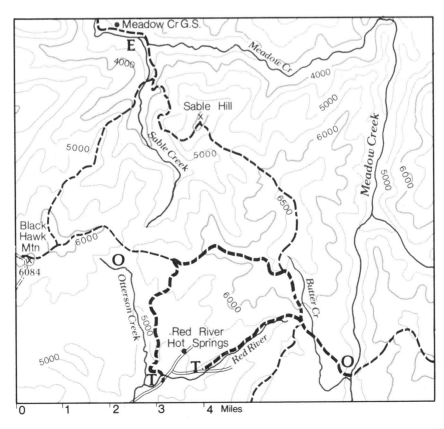

10. Paradise Found

Hikes: D, O, W, E.
Total Distance, W: 14 miles.
Difficulty: Levels I, II.
Season: June 5 – September 15.
Elevation Gain: 900 feet.
USGS Maps: Mt. George, Mt. Paloma,
  Burnt Strip*.
USFS Maps: Selway Bitterroot Wilderness.
Mileage, Lew: 199 (70½ dirt);
  CdA, 287 (36 dirt).

Introduction: Paradise exists right here in Idaho. It lies 12 miles down the Selway River from the Nez Perce Trail Road. All distances east, west, and north are measured in trail miles, for this is the limit of civilization, the major trailhead for the interior of the Selway Bitterroot Wilderness. To the east is the White Cap Creek drainage, to the west Wylies Peak and Running Creek, to the north the Selway River and its many tributaries. The White Cap Creek Trail leads 24 miles east to the Bitterroot Divide. Branches lead up Cooper Creek, to Vance and Paloma Mountains, and on to Darby, Montana. This White Cap trail is Level I all the way to Patsy Ann Falls, 20 miles in. The USFS warns of rattlesnakes below 3500 feet, an elevation the trail doesn't exceed until 5 miles east of Paradise.

The Trail: A good weekender's goal is Cooper Flat, 7 miles in. Overnighters can camp at Cedar and Barefoot Creeks, 4 and 6 miles in. Dayhikers can go up White Cap Creek or down the Selway River, or they can climb 2000 feet to Bad Luck Lookout. The trailhead is well marked, and the eight miles to Cooper Flat go very fast (unless you stop to fish every pool in White Cap Creek). There is one major highlight along the way: the burned area near Baldy Creek. This is a sterling illustration of the USFS's new, enlightened attitude toward fire in wilderness. The Selway-Bitterroot Wilderness has a prescribed burning policy that allows some lightning-caused fires to take their natural course. There are many benefits of this policy. Brush and undergrowth are cleared, making hiking more enjoyable and preventing the buildup

of fuels that can lead to catastrophic fires. Douglas fir seedlings growing in the shade of ponderosa pine are killed. This is good because their dry underbranches, close to the ground, lead to fires' "crowning out" and killing ponderosas, whose thick puzzle bark is highly fire resistant at ground level. Finally, the dense forest canopy is opened up. Watch for the mosaic of live and dead trees across the creek, which provides an ideal mix of forage and cover for game. Enjoy the stretches of trail where the fire burned back "that darned brush." Reject the Smoky Bear mentality politicians have shown in opposing prescribed burning policies. And remember that man's ruthless suppression of wildfires over the past 70 years has created a serious imbalance in forest ecosystems. Wilderness is the ideal place to correct such tampering.

The trail down to Cooper Flat is well signed. You can camp there or continue on the White Cap trail another 2 miles to a large camping area near Paloma Creek. It is in those flats that you get your first glimpses of the mountain fairyland ahead. Near here your author surprised a bear cub, which ran off making shrill sounds translated as "Mammy!" It tried to climb a lodgepole pine, made it up about 8 feet, slid down, ran to the next such tree, and had the same success. Finally disappearing, it left your author whistling to build courage and warn Mammy that he was Man, alleged king of the mountain.

Extensions: You could easily spend two weeks in this drainage. The trail is good all the way to the Triple Lakes. The manway shown to the White Cap Lakes wasn't visible. The trail up to Vance Mountain is crudely signed. Neither trail up to Mt. Paloma was signed.

Access: Follow directions to Magruder Guard Station (page 36). Drive 3¼ miles past its turnoff on the Nez Perce Trail Road, to the Selway River Road. Turn right and drive to Paradise, 12 miles farther. There is no parking at the trailhead at the road's end; park in the USFS campground. The first campsites on the trail come before Wapiti Creek, 1½ miles in.

The Bitterroot Divide at the head of White Cap Creek

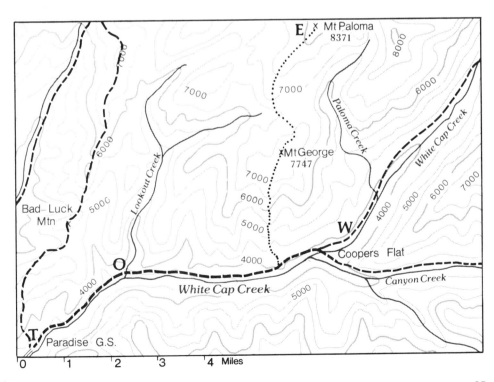

11. The Source of the Selway

Hikes: D, O, W, E.
Total Distance, W: 18 miles.
Difficulty: Level II.
Season: June 1—September 17.
Elevation Gain: 1100 feet.
USGS Maps: Beaver Jack Mountain,
  Wood Hump.
USFS Map: Bitterroot N.F.
Distance, Lew: 190½ (62 dirt);
  CdA: 272 (21 dirt).

Introduction: The River of No Return Wilderness Act extended Wilderness protection to the Selway River south of Magruder Guard Station. Along the 25 miles from Magruder, the Selway is constantly changing. At last, where it flows from Hidden Lake, it is so small you can stand astride it. Unfortunately, the first 9 miles of trail are the poorest of the 25, climbing and descending at the Selway's whim. Past Thompson Flat, the trail becomes less rocky and more even-tempered. Level II to Thompson Flat; Level I beyond.

The Trail: The weekender's goal is Thompson Flat, 9 miles in, where there is lots of camping. Dayhikers can walk until they poop out, while overnighters won't find campsites before Gold Pan and Tepee Creeks, 4 miles in. The well-signed trailhead is almost at the end of the road past the guard station, on the left. Climb the bank and then turn right on the trail of many numbers but one name—the Selway River Trail. It spends a lot of its time above the river, giving you views into pools of extraordinary depth. Campsites start at Gold Pan Creek, and are sprinkled along the way until you come to the big flats at Upper Crossing, where you may spy the remains of an old bridge.

Just across Grass Gulch you pass the last campsite before the river asserts itself and forces the trail to climb. It doesn't descend until the crossing just above Mile 186, where there is a bridge. You meet a few campsites before arriving at Thompson Flat, site of an historic cabin and a magnificent stretch of river. The best camping is near Witter Creek. What seems to be the Goat Ridge Trail climbs just behind the corral.

Extensions: The trail greatly improves at Witter Creek, which is bridged. Just past the creek a trail climbs to the right (Witter Ridge Trail?). There are good campsites before Swet Creek, which does not have a pack bridge and must be forded. A log aids the next crossing of the Selway, which is followed by campsites in a lodgepole flat. The next three crossings, though, must be forded. The third ford is rewarded by the campsites before Camp Creek. There are no campsites from here to the confluence of Stripe, Surprise, and Hidden Creeks, the birthplace of the Selway. Hidden Creek, which flows from Hidden Lake, is the most dramatic headwaters stream. Descend from the signed Stripe Creek Trail to cross Hidden Creek. The sharp bend your map shows is almost imperceptible, and you must watch your compass or the sun to catch this 315° change of course. Watch for Stripe Mountain, with its amazing white band. There are many campsites along the bend area. The USGS map is inaccurate past here. Contour along the 6640 foot level until you come to Hidden Creek. After climbing beside it, you meet the signed Waugh Mountain Trail. Cross the creek and climb the rocky path to Hidden Lake, where there are many campsites.

Access: You can reach Magruder Guard Station via Red River or Darby, Montana. For the Darby route, take US-12 or I-90 east to Lolo or Missoula. Turn right on US-93 and drive 4¼ miles south of Darby to the West Fork Road. Turn right and drive 14½ miles to a turnoff to the right. Take this road to the Magruder Guard Station turnoff, 17½ miles beyond Nez Perce Pass. Turn left and park at the Guard Station. You may car camp in the Deep Creek Campground or along the road to Paradise Guard Station. There are no campsites for the first 4 miles of trail. You can also reach Magruder via Elk City, a shorter route from Lewiston and the one for which the mileage is given. Follow directions for Sheep Hill. The Magruder G.S Road is 31½ slow miles east of Dry Saddle.

Near the source of the Selway

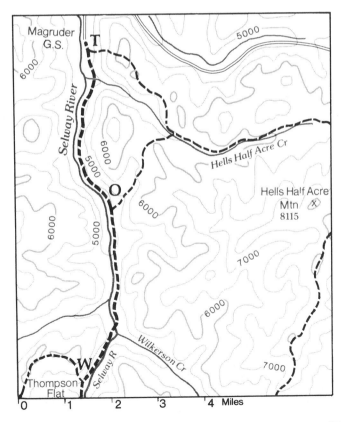

12. To Waugh Mountain

Hikes: D, O, W, E.
Total Distance, W: 18 miles.
Difficulty: Levels I, II.
Season: July 15 — September 15.
Elevation Gain: 1900 feet.
USGS Map: Stripe Mountain.
USFS Map: Bitterroot N.F.; or,
   RNRWA Map.
Mileage, Lew: 172 (59½ dirt).

Introduction: Samuel Parker is one of the most interesting of Idaho's explorers. After receiving a revelation that he should travel West to carry the gospel to the Indians, this sickly Presbyterian minister gained church support, recruited Marcus Whitman to his cause, and journeyed to the Pierre's Hole Rendezvous of 1835. After sending Whitman back East for reinforcements, he rode to Fort Hall with Jim Bridger. Parker then headed north in the company of Nez Perce Indians. Following the Nez Perce Trail, he arrived at Spalding 16 days after his departure from present-day Salmon. For much of his journey, he suffered from a severe illness, and he bled himself three times in 17 days. His book paints a picture of Central Idaho as it was in 1835, is today, and will be forever. This is not a difficult trail unless you cross-country down to Swet Lake; Level I.

The Trail: The weekender's goal is Swet Lake Pond, 9 miles in. Overnighters can stop at Arrow Camp, 4½ miles in, while dayhikers can stop at Devil's Washbasin or Goat Saddle, about 2½ miles from the trailhead at Base Camp. Not long after beginning the hike, you reach a small wonder, a tiny meandering brook. You soon round a corner and climb to the Devils Washbasin view. Snake through this rocky area, passing next to a frog pond. Parker wrote of it, "In one place there were immense quantities of granite, covering more than a hundred acres, in a broken state, as though prepared for making walls, mostly in cubic form." An apt description!

As you leave the Devils Washbasin, you pass under Goat Saddle, from which you can view Salmon Mountain Lookout. As the trail continues on below Goat Mountain, it crosses several creeks, climbs a number of times, and passes some dry camps on the ridge. When you come to the old trail your map shows going straight down to Arrow Camp, go ahead on the newer one, which makes a gentler descent. Arrow Camp is named for an arrow made of wire and embedded in a tree along with the date 7/17/16. There are campsites upstream and downstream from the trail. Continuing on, you effortlessly reach the ridgeline. There is no sign of the Goat Ridge Trail, but the junction at Witter Ridge Campsite is well marked. A spring is just west of the divide, and there are campsites nearby. As you continue southward on the ridge, you pass some dry campsites and then descend to the saddle above the lake at 7464. Another climb and descent bring you to a signed trail divide. Swet Lake Pond, where there is good camping, is just to the left. A small stream flows down to the pond until late summer, but after then water is scarce. Swet Lake is accessed via a path that leaves the pond's northeast corner. It falters near a boulderfield which you cut across to reach the lake. Just past the Pond turnoff is a second trail divide. Swet Lake Cabin is somewhere to the right. The stream your map shows next to the cabin may also run dry in late season.

Extensions: When water is available, the Pond and Cabin make a good base for exploring the surrounding wilderness. To the west, the Dennis Creek Trail is in poor condition. The Harrington Ridge Trail is better, and it accesses East Dennis Lake. To the south, you will find water before and after Swet Point. From Eakin Point you have your choice of trails, one of which continues on Parker's route over fabulous Waugh Mountain to Waugh Lake.

Access: Follow directions to Dry Saddle (page 40). Beyond there you enter the West Fork Ranger District's nether regions, and the road is poorly maintained. You will do well to average fifteen miles an hour in this area. Base Camp is 13¼ miles east of Dry Saddle and 15 miles west of the Paradise Road. While the trailhead doesn't make appetizing camping, there is a good campground at Chuckling Creek, 4 miles east. The first campsites on the trail come on the ridge above Arrow Camp, 3½ miles in.

On the Nez Perce Trail

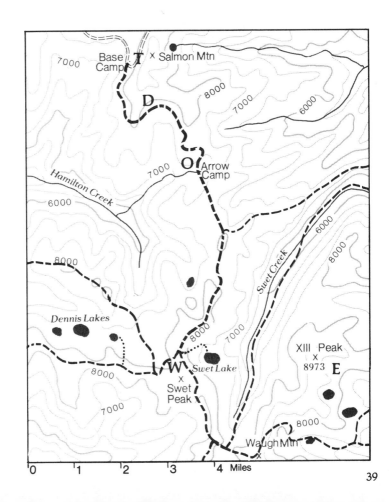

13. Sheep Hill

Hikes: D, O, W, E.
Total Distance, W: 14 miles.
Difficulty: Level II+.
Season: July 20—September 15.
Elevation Gain: 2400 feet.
USGS Maps: Sabe Mountain*,
   Spread Creek Point, Sheep Hill.
USFS Maps: Nez Perce N.F.; or,
   RNRWA Map.
Mileage, Lew: 158½ (32 dirt).

Introduction: "Salmon River Breaks" was a good description of the old Primitive Area that was incorporated into the River of No Return Wilderness Area. It consisted of several north-south ridges arrayed on the Salmon's north side. Sheep Hill Lookout is at the southern end of one of these ridges, nine tough miles from the Nez Perce Trail Road. It is three air miles from the Salmon, and 6000 feet above it. This is a real "bear went over the mountain" trail. It follows the ridgeline relentlessly, climbing right to the summits of the peaks. As you hike south on it, you pass many lakes whose waters feed the two great creeks on either side—Bargamin and Sabe. The trail is rugged and rocky but easy to follow: Level II+.

The Trail: The weekender's goal is Lake Creek Lakes, 7 miles in. Dayhikers and overnighters can choose from the three Trilby Lakes, 1 mile; Spread Point Lake, 3 miles; or Saddle Lake, 5 miles in. Start by hiking on an old road until you see the trailhead register box, your first landmark. From here you descend the right flank of the ridge to a view of the Trilby Lakes. As is the case with Spread Point Lake, there is no signed trail down to the lake.

After you have passed Spread Creek Point, with its curious old lookout structure, you come to a signed trail junction above Saddle Creek Lake. The trail down to the lake is marked, as is the Ring Creek Trail. Turn right at this divide and you will shortly enjoy a panoramic view of the upper Ring Creek. From the saddle below you could cut left and find a campsite near the marsh your map shows. One more climb on the trail, to 8145, prepares you for the descent to the Lake

Creek Lakes (called the Sheep Lakes on some maps). As you lose altitude you pass some excellent springs. The trail to the lakes turns right just past the creek that feeds the lower lake. The lakes basin is large and level. It should be easy to follow wilderness rules requiring that your camp be at least 200 feet away from water.

If you wish to go farther, you must negotiate the trail junction that comes a short climb past the lakes. It is as confusing as the USGS map implies. To reach Sheep Hill Lookout, take the rightmost trails. At Dead Man Saddle, an old grave is just to the right. Sheep Hill has a superb view of the RNRWA. One of the old Idaho Primitive Area's most remote areas, the southern portion of the Salmon River Breaks, lies just "across the street." To the southeast lie Cottonwood Butte before, and the Big Horn Crags beyond, the Middle Fork of the Salmon. The tall peaks south of Big Creek and those west of Chamberlain Basin are also visible, as is the Salmon River itself.

Extensions: Bear Point and the Center Mountain Lakes beckon. They are southeast of the confusing intersection.

Access: Drive south on US-95 from Spalding to Grangeville, 65½ miles. Turn left and drive 1¼ miles through town to the Grangeville-Salmon Road. Turn right, and then left after another ¾ mile. Drive through Mt. Idaho to the South Fork Clearwater River (ID-14). Follow the river for 36 miles, to Elk City Junction. Turn right and drive 14 miles to Red River Ranger Station. Go straight for a long ¼ mile, and then turn left on the Nez Perce Trail Road. After 1¾ more miles turn right. The next crucial turn comes 1¾ miles past Granite Springs (good water to the right of the road), where you turn right. When the long climb from Bargamin Creek ends, you are at Dry Saddle. Park along the main road: don't try the 50 yards of "road" that lead to the parking area. You can camp on the ridge just south of here, or at Mountain Meadows, Granite Springs, or Poet Camp along the Nez Perce Trail Road.

The Salmon River Breaks

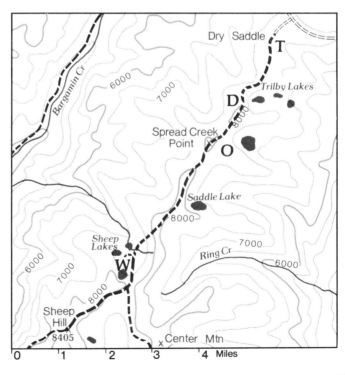

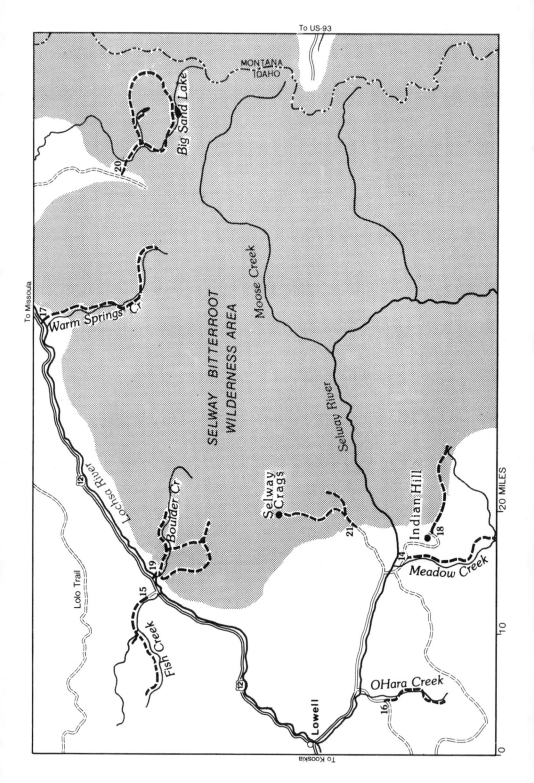

To US-93

MONTANA
IDAHO

Big Sand Lake

20

To Missoula

Warm Springs Cr.
17

SELWAY BITTERROOT
WILDERNESS AREA

Moose Creek

Lochsa River

Selway River

12

Boulder Cr.

Selway Crags

21

Indian Hill

18

19

Meadow Creek

4

Lolo Trail

Fish Creek

15

OHara Creek

12

Lowell

16

To Kooskia

20 MILES

10

0

Smooth Water, Rough Water

In the Flathead tongue, Selway means "smooth water" and Lochsa means "rough water." These two great rivers drain one of America's finest Wildernesses, the Selway Bitterroot. Almost one-and-a-half million acres in size, with Idaho elevations ranging from 1800 near Selway Falls to 9012 on the Bitterroot Divide, the Selway is a wilderness par excellence. Large tracts have been set aside as "pristine areas" with no trail maintenance, and this is good. But most other trails aren't maintained very well, either! Few were built with gentle grades or water bars; all too many simply follow ridgelines, and heavy horse use has resulted in severe erosion. Forest Service experts, when queried about such multiple-rutted trails, respond "But this is wilderness." The author agrees in part, but he cannot accept those ugly scars, and believes that many trails must be rebuilt so that they will endure, and so hikers can experience the entirely legitimate joy of walking on a good wilderness trail. If the experts are so bent on making the hikers' backcountry travel unpleasant, why don't they import some hostile Native Americans to harass the campers? *That* would really make for an old-time wilderness experience!

The Selway Bitterroot Wilderness is sparsely covered by this book; only six weekend hikes are described in an area where one could easily roam for a month. (There are too many hard-to-find, non-wilderness areas in Idaho to dwell at length on the Selway, which everyone knows about.) The author would be hard pressed to recommend any one part of the Selway to visit on an extended trip. Perhaps the best approach for route selection would be to play pin-the-tail-on-the-donkey with the wilderness area map. After you have thus picked a goal, choose the most roundabout way of reaching it. Based on the author's personal experience, if you don't go during hunting season you will meet very, very few people...

The Forest Service has printed a useful pamphlet called the *Selway Bitterroot Wilderness Primer;* when you write or stop for maps or information, request a copy.

The Lochsa, a Wild River, is highly regarded by kayakers and float trippers, and provides many fine views for drivers on the winding highway that parallels it. That road, US-12, is a main corridor for heavily laden grain trucks, ponderous recreation vehicles, and cross-country bicyclists. A recent controversy over the highway was resolved in favor of improving it. The changes will probably make it more safe for humans but more dangrous for animals. When you drive US-12, be sure to stop at the Lochsa Historic Ranger Station for a glimpse of Forest Service life in the old days when trails were maintained.

14. Meadow Creek

Hikes: D, W, E.
Total Distance, W: 16 miles.
Difficulty: Level I.
Season: March 15—September 15.
Elevation Gain: 1700 feet.
USGS Maps: Selway Falls,
   Anderson Butte.
USFS Maps: Nez Perce N.F.; or
   Selway Bitterroot Wilderness.
Mileage, Lew: 104 (14 dirt).

Introduction: The Selway River Trail is a major thoroughfare during the summer. The Meadow Creek Trail, which has very similiar qualities, is much less used, simply because it is not part of a designated wilderness area. In its forty mile course Meadow Creek, the Selway's biggest tributary, drains a large roadless area. The River of No Return Wilderness Act opened this area to multiple use management, ignoring the effects logging might have on its important steelhead spawning areas. And the logging to be done in upper Meadow Creek was justified on the basis of only two factors: the value of the trees, and the cost of cutting them. No consideration was given to watershed, wildlife, fisheries, recreation, or the ability of the forest to regenerate itself. Is this the shape "cost-benefit analysis" will take in the future? This hike covers lower Meadow Creek, an excellent early season hike on a National Recreation Trail. Middle Meadow Creek can be reached from Red River Hot Springs, while the sources of the creek in Mountain Meadows (soon to be logged) can be seen from the Nez Perce Trail Road. The trail is generally easy to hike; Level I.

The Trail: The weekender's goal is the Lark Creek area, 8 miles in. Dayhikers can stop anywhere as far as the start of the climb, 3 miles in. Overnighters are warned that campsites are few in that three mile stretch and none for the next five miles. The trailhead is easy to locate. If you hike this trail in the spring, your first reaction may be, this is a *creek*? Indeed, Meadow Creek is as big as a river. From the trailhead to Little Creek those campsites you encounter are uneven and near to the trail. But every view is special due to this marvelous creek.

A fine stand of cedars marks the beginning of the thousand foot climb. This is not a typical case of a streamside trail climbing and then losing altitude unnecessarily (and annoyingly). By the time you descend to the creek, it will have gained 600 of those 1000 feet back. Once you have climbed, you enter an exciting, changing world. You proceed from warm southern exposures with views of the green hills to come, to beautiful side creeks complete with falls, and then on to cool northern exposures with occasional glimpses of snowcapped peaks north of the Selway. Along the way, in two places, the creek narrows to less than forty feet (where it is shown on the USGS map as a single line). Both these turbulent stretches are visible from the trail. A final, drier stretch brings you to the junction with the Indian Hill Trail, from which you descend to Indian Hill and Meadow Creeks. Campsites are plentiful on this stretch of Meadow Creek, especially in the large flat by Lark Creek.

Extensions: The Meadow Creek drainage is well trailed. Loop hikes can be made via the Vermilion and Buck Lake Creek Trails, or on the Anderson Butte side of the creek.

Access: Drive 84 miles on US-12 from Spalding Junction to the Selway River Road at Lowell. Turn right and drive 18¾ miles to the Selway Falls Bridge. Turn right again, and drive up Meadow Creek to the trailhead, which is just across the Meadow Creek bridge and to the right. There is a USFS campground on Meadow Creek, and a few campsites on the first three miles of trail.

Cedars at the base of the climb

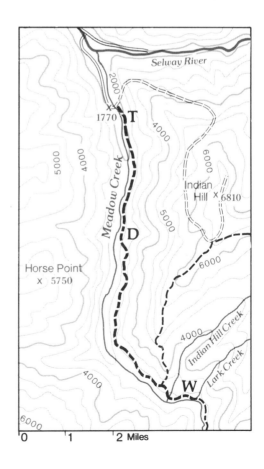

15. Fish Creek

Hikes: D, O, W, E.
Total Distance, W: 16 miles.
Difficulty: Levels I, II.
Season: March 15 — September 20.
Elevation Gain: 1100 feet.
USGS Maps: Huckleberry Butte,
  McLendon Butte.
USFS Maps: Clearwater N.F.
Mileage, Lew: 108 (¾ dirt).

Introduction: Most of the Lochsa River's tributaries from the south rise in the Selway Bitterroot Wilderness. But what of those to the north? Do any flow from areas of similar untrammeled wilderness? The answer is yes, spelled F-I-S-H. Fish Creek drains a large roadless area that, like much of the wilderness to the south, is recovering from devastating wildfire. This recovery proceeds at wildly varying rates, creating a patchwork of dark green forest, light green brush, and every shade in between. The real winners in the process are the elk and deer that are numerous here. The Fish Creek Trail is in good Level I condition for its first seven miles; it then deteriorates to Level II.

The Trail: The weekender's goal is the clearing 7 miles up Fish Creek; overnighters can stop anywhere up to Obia Cabin, 4½ miles in; while dayhikers can stop at Willow Creek, 3 miles in. The trailhead is well marked. There are a few campsites in the first 3 miles of trail, as you pass Pondosa and Pagoda Creeks. Now, 15 years after the USGS maps were compiled, would you show the vegetation on the other side of Fish Creek as woodlands (solid green) or brush (stippled green pattern)? Good camping starts in the flats just below Willow Creek (which is bridged) and continues for ½ mile. The USFS requests no camping next to Obia Cabin, which perhaps should be renamed "Obia Shack."

There are suitable sites across the bridge and to the right along Hungery Creek, near the island shown on your USGS map. Lewis and Clark passed this way in 1804 and 1805, camping on and naming Hungery Creek.

Before Fish Creek joins Hungery, it must drop 240 feet. It does this in a mere half mile, creating a torrent of foaming white water, and causing a large rockslide on the stream's south side. When you have climbed above these falls, you enter a long level area with many campsites, the weekender's goal. From here to Ceanothus Creek the trail worsens. It varies from the USGS map, always staying low and near to the creek. There are more campsites along the way to Ceanothus.

Extensions: There is no sign of the Fish Creek Trail's crossing Fish Creek just before Ceanothus Creek, as your USGS map shows. Nor does the Hungery Creek Trail shown on new USFS maps look promising. The trail up to Ant Hill is in good condition.

Access: Drive 84 miles up US-12 from Spalding Junction to Lowell, and then another 23 miles to the Fish Creek Road (just across the bridge). The trailhead is ¾ mile up the road, along which there are several campsites (with Wilderness Gateway Campground three miles up the highway). There are a few campsites along the trail's first 1½ miles.

Where tall trees once stood

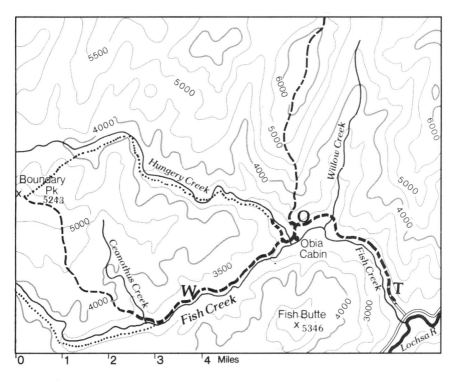

16. O'Hara Creek

Hikes: D, O, W.
Total Distance, O: 11 miles.
Difficulty: Levels I, III.
Season: April 15 – September 20.
Elevation Gain: 2100 feet.
USGS Maps: Iron Mtn., Goddard Point.
USFS Map: Nez Perce N.F.
Mileage, Lew: 95 (4 dirt).

Introduction: Like many other tributaries to the Selway, O'Hara Creek is trailed because it is simply too steep to road. And like Meadow, Gedney, Glover and other non-wilderness creeks, the trail going up O'Hara Creek is little used. It has a most changeable nature and provides good camping from early to late season. The first 1½ miles of trail are easy going, Level I; the next 4½ miles are rough going and Level III.

The Trail: Overnighters can camp either along lower O'Hara Creek in the first 1½ miles of trail, or on the upper East Fork, 5½ miles in. Dayhikers can push beyond the first crossing (1½ miles) if they wish. The hike no longer starts at 2272 as shown on your map. Instead, a new contouring trail begins down the road at a sign that may be partially obscured by brush. This excellent trail passes above possible campsites in the shadow of big cedars, and by the murmur/roar of the creek. The crossing of Hamby Fork is facilitated by an old cedar log with a handline. The first crossing of O'Hara Creek is just beyond. This must be forded in early season, but later you can use the logs downstream.

From here on, the trail deteriorates. It is brushy, ferny, eroding away, and hard to follow. The second crossing of O'Hara follows a short rocky stretch of trail, where you see a small island in the creek. This, too, is a ford. Route finding problems continue on the other side of the creek. Watch for the switchback your map shows, and be careful on the slickrock stretches. Be sure you stop to take in all the different moods of this marvelous creek: meek and narrow; loud and rocky; powerfully falling. Perhaps the huge cedar log your author encountered will still block the trail, bereft of bark, marred by the claw and hoof marks of animals that have clambered over its great girth. You may wish you had claws, too!

When you reach the forks of O'Hara Creek, you will be chagrined to find that the fork you must ford, the West Fork, is the larger of the two. But once you have crossed, you will be pleased to find that the trail has vastly improved. It climbs easily through a young cedar forest. The two streams your USGS map shows the trail crossing at 4200 feet mark the first campsites above the forks, in a big meadow.

Access: Drive to Lowell, 84 miles east of Spalding on US-12. Turn right on the Selway River Road and drive 7 miles to the O'Hara Creek Bridge at the end of the pavement. Turn right. Your trailhead is 4 miles up the road. You can camp in the first 1½ miles of trail, or in the campground next to the bridge.

A creek of many moods

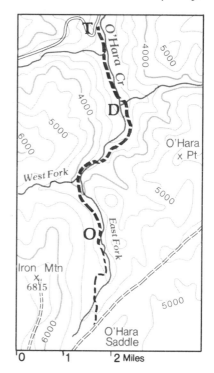

17. Warm Springs Creek

Hikes: D, O, W, E.
Difficulty: Levels, I, II.
Total Distance, W: 14 miles.
Season: May 15 — September 15.
Elevation Gain: 1700 feet.
USGS Maps: Tom Beal Peak, Bear Mtn*.
USFS Map: Selway Bitterroot Wilderness.
Mileage, Lew: 139 (no dirt).

Introduction: From its source in a paradise of grey granite, green meadows, and glittering white snow, Warm Springs Creek flows twenty miles to the Lochsa River. It ever repeats a cycle of pools, riffles, meanders, and falls. The creek has an excellent trail system, with loop routes limited only by one's imagination. The trail is Level I to the ford, Level II thereafter.

The Trail: Dayhikers and overnighters can hike to the excellent cedar groves beyond Jerry Johnson Hot Springs, about 2 miles in. Weekenders can reach the lodgepole flats at Wind Lakes Creek, 7 miles in. The trail bears right across the bridge and proceeds to the hot springs, where about 95% of its users stop. Like many other wilderness hot springs, this one attracts all sorts of people, and unpleasant incidents have occurred. Stay away! Once past the hot springs, human impacts decrease rapidly, and there are many excellent campsites in the cedars.

Well, all good things must come to an end, Warm Springs Creek must reach its sources at 7000 feet, and you can't hike on level ground forever! Excellent switchbacks help you climb well above the creek, to a fine view of its biggest falls. A while later, you pass a smaller falls. The area around Wind Lakes Creek's confluence is a vast lodgepole flats with limitless camping possibilities.

Extensions: Until mid-July, your only option from here is to ascend Wind Lakes Creek, because the ford is as bad as it looks. Later, you can cross and continue up Warm Springs Creek. There are campsites before and beyond the second ford, which is easier than it looks. When the creek makes its cut to the south, the trail becomes wet and boggy. A climb to the right brings you almost to Hungry Lake. A turn to the left brings you to the cirque that gives birth to this fabulous creek.

Access: Drive 84 miles east of Spalding Junction on US-12 to Lowell, and then 55 miles further to the "Trail 49" sign at the packbridge. There are many USFS campgrounds along the highway, and campsites 2 miles down the trail.

The upper falls

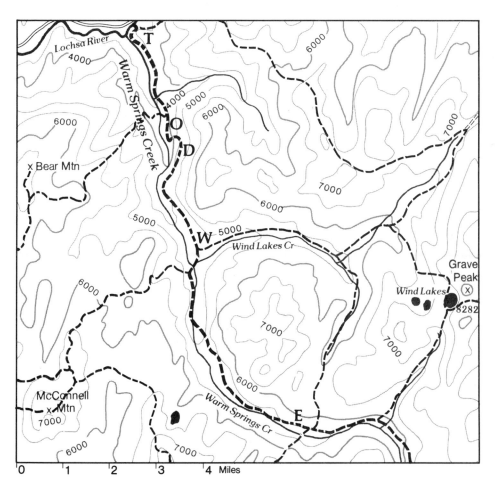

18. Indian Hill

Hikes: D, W, E.
Total Distance, W: 20 miles.
Difficulty: Level I.
Season: July 4 – September 15.
Elevation Gain: 3800 feet.
USGS Maps: Vermilion Peak,
  Running Lake*.
USFS Map: Selway Bitterroot
  Wilderness
Mileage, Lew: 116 (26 dirt).

Introduction: South and west of the Selway River, the Selway Bitterroot Wilderness Area is dominated by ridges, peaks, meadows, and lakes. Indian Hill, with a manned lookout tower, anchors the western end of this area and serves as jumping-off point for expeditions to it. This trail was recently rebuilt to high standards. Instead of following ridges and eroding into multiple ruts, it sidehills from meadow to meadow, enjoying moderate grades and southern exposures. The cost of such trail reconstruction in time, money, and manpower is obviously great (this one needed some two man-years). So, one must ask, why doesn't the USFS put more effort into maintaining the trails it has now, so it doesn't have to similarly reconstruct every trail in ten years? This is a good trail, rated Level I.

The Trail: Weekenders can reach Buck Lake, 10 miles, or the meadow east of Little Copper Butte, 7½ miles. Dayhikers can climb Copper Butte, while overnighters seem out of luck here. After a short stretch of old road, the trail meets a junction where you can turn right for Indian Park. It gradually descends to Mica Creek Saddle, passing water on the way, and then climbs via switchback. At about 6400 you come to the last water for four miles. You then contour under Copper and Little Copper Buttes. There are possible campsites and dubious water south of Little Copper, and good campsites near to and far from the trail northeast of Little Copper. There is good water on the trail about 5 minutes past the northeast meadow, right under 7130. The Highline Ridge Trail junction is signed, and Drake Saddle, with its view down Mink Creek, is big enough to dry camp at.

All that's left is the climb and descent to Buck Lake, where horses have been banned (now that they've trampled down the vegetation, leaving nice cleared campsites). These sites are located north and south of the lake, and there is a good water source to the west.

Extensions: Fawn Lake is hard to reach, Doe Lake easier. Indian Park is an historic Nez Perce campsite. Red Lake, Mink Peak, and Bilk Mountain all beckon!

Access: Same as Meadow Creek Trail (page 44), except turn left when you cross the Meadow Creek Bridge. The Indian Hill Road was once a good one, and a little maintenance would go a long way. However, at present it is best suited to rugged cars with clearance, maneuverability, and manual transmissions. The trailhead is 12 miles from the bridge, and there are dry campsites there. The first possible campsites on the trail are dry ones on the south flank of Copper Butte, 3 miles in.

Vermillion Peak

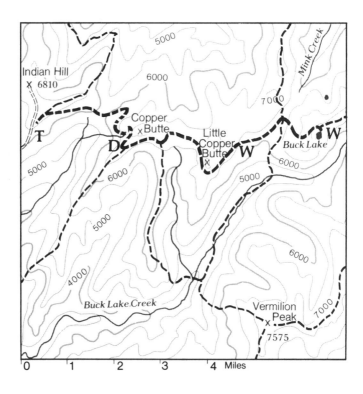

19. Boulder Creek Trails

Hikes: D, O, W, E.
Total Distance, W: 28 miles.
Difficulty: Levels I, II.
Season: April 15—September 15.
Elevation Gain: 5000 feet.
USGS Maps: Huckleberry Butte,
 Greenside Butte*.
USFS Map: Selway Bitterroot Wilderness.
Mileage, Lew: 111 (no dirt).

Introduction: Boulder Creek provides a quick introduction to the Selway Bitterroot Wilderness's ecosystems, awesome scenics, and awful problems. Elevations range from 2100 to 7300 feet, with vegetational patterns further diversified by fires which have left large brushy areas. Cliff and Surprise Creeks' valleys are easy to eyeball, while high points such as Huckleberry Butte give fine views of the Selway Crags. And on popular routes like these, hikers and horsemen meet frequently on eroded trails. The dusty trail to Horse Camp is generally Level I; the loop up to Maud and Lottie Lakes and down Huckleberry Butte is Level II. Boil all your water.

The Trails: Dayhikers should head towards Lochsa Saddle, 4 miles on Trail 220, the Huckleberry Butte Trail. Overnighters must go 5½ miles to reach campsites on Trail 211, the Boulder Creek Trail. Weekenders can reach Horse Camp, 9 miles in on Trail 211, while those with more time or energy can reach the Maud and Lottie Lakes area and loop out over Huckleberry Butte, 28 miles. The trailhead area has changed much since your USGS map was published; consult campground bulletin boards for an area map. Trail 211 starts next to the twin bridges, new and old, while Trail 220 begins directly across from the entrance to the new trailhead parking area. The Boulder Creek Trail commences with a switchback, but otherwise follows the USGS map on its way to first water from the creek under Lone Knob. Aside from a new short cut to the Boulder Creek ford, the trail junction at 3443 is as shown on your map. You can camp there, but the best sites are dry ones up Trail 211, to the left after a climb. The trail on to Horse Camp is as shown, passing meadows and campsites.

Trail 221 crosses the ford and leads to the high country. Despite its "infrequent maintenance" status, despite the (alleged) closure of Maud and Lottie Lakes to horses, despite the heavy foot traffic it receives, despite its poor design and total lack of erosion control, and despite the proximity of the "frequent maintenance" Surprise Creek Trail, Trail 221 is open to horses. It now meets Trail 222 next to 4171, but otherwise follows the USGS map on the way to the junction with the Huckleberry Butte Trail. Turn left there. Your USGS and USFS maps misname the lakes: Maud is the western one, Lottie the eastern one. There is no reason to camp near them, for the area abounds with dispersed, dry campsites. They are found off the trail that heads southwest from the area between the two lakes; before you reach the upper lake at 6359; and on the ridge that forms the south boundary of this lakes basin.

Best exit from this area is by Trail 220. It offers good views from Huckleberry Butte, freedom from horses, and a cool, shady descent. Go straight at the junction west of the lakes, discover the "switch-ups" near the 6060 foot saddle, and crawl to the top of Huckleberry. It's all downhill from here! The descent west of Cantaloupe Peak is rocky. But from Lochsa Saddle down, the trail is perfect, with good grades, good tread, good shade, and good water. The water is just west of the saddle.

Extensions: The trail is rocky from Horse Camp to Fish Lake Saddle, and rockier from there to Two Lakes. It improves to Shasta Lake (camp in meadow below lake), then deteriorates over Stanley Butte and past the Seven Lakes. The Cliff Creek Trail is boggy, hard to follow, and poorly mapped. Trail 222 is a tough, dry hike, but likely horse-free.

Access: Same as Fish Creek (page 46), but proceed 3 miles past its turnoff and turn right at Wilderness Gateway. Drive across the second bridge and park in the trailhead parking area. No campsites on Trail 211 for 5½ miles, but Wilderness Gateway is a fine developed campground.

The head of Old Man Creek

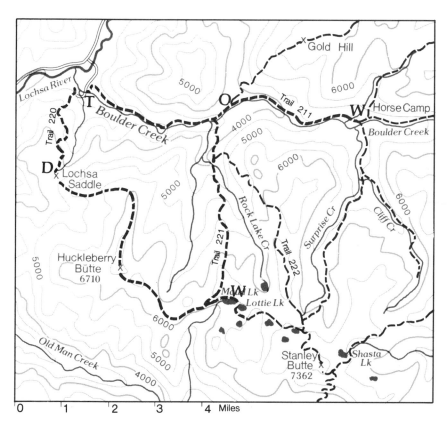

20. Big Lakes Loop

Hikes: D, O, W, E.
Total Distance, W: 23 miles.
Difficulty: Levels I, II.
Season: July 4–September 15.
Elevation Gain: 4300 feet.
USGS Maps: Jeanette Mountain,
  Savage Ridge*, Blodgett Mountain.
USFS Map: Selway Bitterroot Wilderness
  Area.
Mileage, Lew: 168 (15¼ dirt).

Introduction: East of Elk Summit, west of the Bitterroot Divide — here lies an area of surpassing beauty, variety, and challenge. This loop passes two large, lower elevation lakes with trout and two small, higher elevation lakes without. Such barren lakes provide an enjoyable change of pace, eliminating the "need" to fish and giving you a chance to explore other aspects of wilderness. (After all, untrammeled mountain lakes rarely have fish in them.) The trail to the big lakes is Level I; the loop route is steeper and rougher, Level II.

The Trails: Dayhikers and overnighters can reach the fords, 2½ miles from the road. Weekenders can hike to either Hidden Lake, 8 miles in, or to Big Sand Lake, 10 miles in. The 23 mile loop is best hiked counterclockwise, so you can go downhill on the best trail and climb on the worst. Start by descending the Bridge Creek Trail. It passes beautiful meadows, climbs thrice to avoid boggy stretches, and meets two fords: the first an easy crossing of Bridge Creek, the second a harder crossing of deeper Big Sand Creek. Once on the other side, hike south on a good trail that passes many campsites. If you are going directly to Hidden Lake, use an unsigned, unmapped, but well blazed cutoff trail that starts just one minute before you reach the Hidden Creek ford. To hike the loop, cross that ford and continue up Big Sand. Just past another ford, you meet the trail from Elk Summit. While the maps show the trail again crossing Big Sand upstream from a pond, the best ford is the first you meet, below the pond. Once across the creek, stay on the north side all the way to Big Sand Lake. There are campsites by its inlet.

To continue on the loop, climb from the trail junction just past the lake. This trail has many switchbacks not shown on your map. Descend from the summit to another trail junction. The Hidden Lake Trail, rarely maintained, leads to the left. Frog Lake and stunning scenery are to the right. In early season parts of the Frog Lake trail are pre-empted by the headwaters of Hidden Creek. When you reach a broad ridgetop, turn left and climb to the right of 7827. A series of tight switchbacks help you descend from there to Frog Lake, where there are many campsites. The route down to Tadpole Lake has a super-wild character. You may well encounter snow as you climb and descend Frog Peak. Heed well the USGS map and turn right, following curious blaze *signs*, when you come to the meadow north of the Peak. As you traverse under Hidden Peak, fill your canteens in the creeks you cross. From there on, you hike through delightful lodgepole forest.

Hidden Lake is visible from the main trail, and you should have no trouble spotting the unsigned trail that descends to it. The first campsite at Hidden Lake is a horsepacker's heaven and a backpacker's hell. Continue past this dungheap and find a decent spot further along the shore. Past the Hidden Lake junction, the main trail meets a creek with a campsite. It then contours along the ridgeside for a while, cutting across several creeks before beginning a long stately descent to Hidden Creek. Turn right on the cutoff trail and then right on the Big Sand Trail to complete your loop.

Extensions: You could cut north off Hidden Creek Ridge and head for the White Sand Creek country. Or you could explore the Dead Elk Creek and Blodgett Mountain area south of Big Sand Lake.

Access: Drive 154 miles east of Spalding Junction on US-12, to the Elk Summit Road. Turn right, and go straight after crossing the Lochsa bridge. Two and a half miles from the highway, turn left on a poor dirt road, which you follow 12¾ more miles to the Bridge Creek trailhead. Elk Summit Guard Station is 1¾ miles farther, and you should check in there to get current trail information. You can camp near the Bridge Creek ford, 2½ miles in on that trail; or along the road before or beyond the guard station.

Big Flat Creek

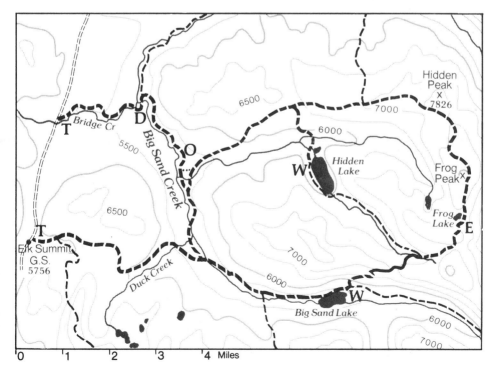

21. The Selway Crags

Hikes: D, O, W, E.
Difficulty: Levels II, III.
Total Distance, W: 16 miles.
Season: July 4 – September 15.
Elevation Gain: 3200 feet.
USGS Maps: Fenn Mountain,
  Fog Mountain*.
USFS Map: Selway Bitterroot Wilderness
  Area.
Mileage, Lew: 114½ (24 dirt).

Introduction: If your Uncle Horace resembles a mountain goat, then perhaps you have the genetic makeup to challenge Idaho's most rugged backcountry area. Trails in the Selway Crags mostly go up or down, often at a scary pace. In the rare moments when they are level, they are usually in a bog. They are poorly built and poorly maintained, and the author found his usual two-miles-per-hour pace cut in half. Good campsites are scarce, and you may have to accept one lower and wetter, higher and drier, or rougher and farther than you like. The popular trail to Cove Lakes and the dayhike to Big Fog Mountain are Level II, but all other trails and routes are Level III.

The Trail: Dayhikers should climb to Big Fog Mountain, 2½ miles in, while overnighters can drop into Canteen Meadows, 4½ miles. Weekenders can stay in Canteen Meadows, at Cove Lakes (6 miles), or near Rainbow Lake (8 miles). Start all hikes with a full canteen, for the area can get quite dry in late summer. The Cove Lakes Trail descends west from the trailhead, quickly entering a landscape that still bears the scars of the great fire of 1934. There are several campsites up majestic Canteen Creek. Your USGS map accurately portrays the climb and descent to Cove Lakes. Use a campstove to avoid further denudation of the area (from which packstock has now been banned). The best campsites are to the north of the upper lake, where your USGS map shows a trail that isn't there. The trail really descends to Gedney Creek, where there is some camping. It then climbs a brushy hillside, and at a stand of trees meets the route that climbs to Jesse Pass. The main trail then bears left to Rainbow Lake's outlet stream, by which there are a few campsites. There is little camping at Rainbow Lake.

The Canteen Meadows trail is not maintained. It climbs up a mostly barren ridge to Big Fog Mountain, from which you can view the Selway Crags. Distances are deceptive here – ridges made of similar rock blend together and look closer than they are, while small, young trees appear to be farther away. Canteen Meadows is reached via the saddle at 6795. There are campsites on the granite sheet around 6200 feet. You could exit by crossing the creek and descending the 6424 ridge to the Cove Lakes Trail.

Extensions: Past Cove Lakes all trails and routes require expert skills. Worst of all is the trail from Old Man Lake to Old Man Meadows. It is OK as far as the saddle at 5640 (the safest access to Lloyd Lake), but the descent from there to the Meadows is deadly steep. Don't try it. You can also try the east side of the Crags, reached from Jesse Pass. That pass can be reached via the Cove Lakes Trail or the ridge north of Big Fog Mountain. This is a pristine, super-rugged wilderness and must be treated with immense respect. Here the two-edged sword of Survival becomes especially keen: if your skill level isn't high enough to let you leave the environment in mint condition, it isn't high enough to let you depart it alive.

Access: The road is almost as bad as the trail: so steep your author's brakes faded on the way down; so rocky and rutted another hiker's flywheel housing was holed. Follow directions for O'Hara Creek (page 48), except drive 11¾ miles past the O'Hara Creek Road, to the Selway Falls Guard Station. Check in there, and drive ¼ mile back to the Fog Mountain Road. There are campsites eight and nine miles up the road and at the trailhead, 12 miles up. First campsites on the trail are on Canteen Creek.

Fenn Mountain, 8021

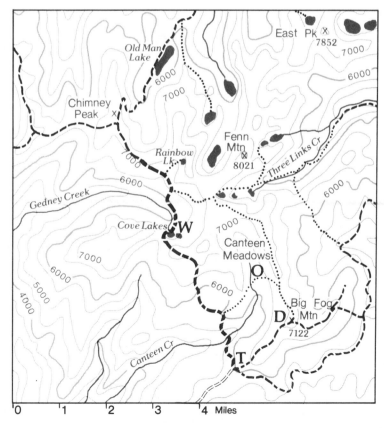

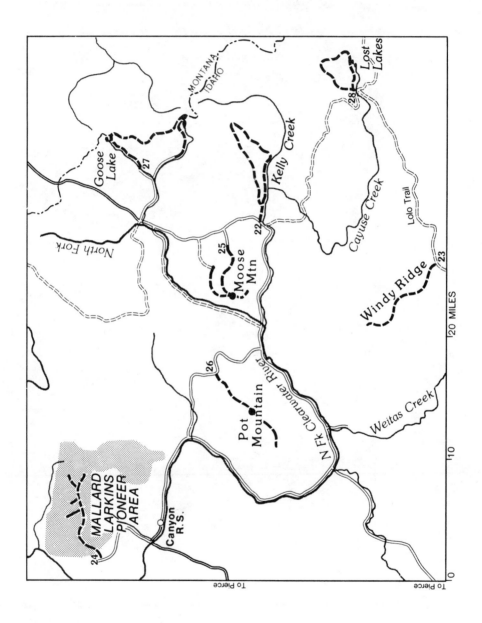

Around the Black Canyon

The Clearwater River's North Fork drains five significant backcountry areas. The Mallard Larkins Pioneer Area lies north of the river and stretches all the way to the St Joe. The Pot Mountain-Elizabeth Lakes area is nestled in a great bend the river makes from Canyon to Bungalow to Kelly Creek to The Cedars. Weitas Creek drains a large roadless area to the south. Moose Mountain is a small and little visited island of high country east of the Clearwater's Black Canyon. And along the Idaho-Montana border lies the spectacular Big Burn/Hoodoo area.

Wilderness is needed in this region to preserve its glories from the merciless style and relentless pace of logging, North Idaho style. From Mallard-Larkins you look south to a sea of huge clearcuts; one clearcut near Pot Mountain covers some 800 acres. Private lands in the area are treated with even less respect, and the need for access to private lands may impact public wilderness. Travel on the region's roads requires extreme prudence, with a CB radio recommended to advise you of approaching logging trucks.

Where man has not toyed with it, the area's environment is extraordinarily rich and varied. There are high country areas such as the Bitterroot Divide almost stripped of trees by the great fires, ridges such as Mallard-Larkins studded with huge hemlocks, and remnants of pre-fire days such as the heritage Cedar Grove. Wildlife loves this area, and elk, moose, and deer abound. The Mallard-Larkins upland has a large mountain goat population which is renowned for its lack of fear of man. Many grizzly bear sightings have been reported in the Kelly Creek and Pot Mountain areas. This is also wolf country! Numerous reports have come from Windy Ridge and Kelly Creek, and the wolf population is probably breeding. At present this is high quality wild country that richly rewards the toil and sweat that hikers invest in it.

The Forest Service's Northern Region Plan provides a disturbing picture of the future for this and other North Idaho backcountry areas. Funding for logging roads is to be trebled by 1990, and by the year 2000 60% of the timber harvest will be on lands presently roadless. Dispersed recreation will be drastically reduced. Developed recreation is *supposed* to increase. But the 1981 Black Canyon Environmental Assessment gave a preview of coming non-attractions. New logging road construction seems to have soaked up too much money to allow construction of much-needed campgrounds. Although there will be closures of main roads for five years, large recreation benefits are claimed that will offset road construction costs! Forest Service suggestions for relieving increased pressure on the native cutthroat fishery include closing the few campsites that exist. And worst of all, the Forest Supervisor selected the plan without even considering public input. Continued emphasis on Timber as the only resource worth managing can only damage the environment of the North Fork. There must be change!

22. Kelly Creek

Hikes: D, O, W, E.
Total Distance, W: 14 miles.
Difficulty: Levels I, II.
Season: May 15 – September 30.
Elevation Gain: 3500 feet.
USGS Maps: Gorman Hill, Toboggan
    Ridge, Straight Peak* (1:62,500).
USFS Map: Clearwater N.F.
Mileage, Lew: 130 (42 dirt).

Introduction: Kelly Creek is the major stream that drains the Big Burn Wilderness, and it is a fabulous one. Unfortunately, this entire 18 mile loop was excluded from the RARE II wilderness proposal. The Kelly Creek Trail is still in good, Level I condition. The Little Moose Ridge and Bruin Hill Trails have some rough stretches that are getting worse: Level II.

The Trails: Weekenders have several choices starting at Bear Meadows, 7 miles in. Overnighters and dayhikers can stop near Cayuse Creek, 3½ miles in. The Kelly Creek Trail has been built to high standards, and after a quick climb from the signed trailhead it proceeds at a steady grade. As you zip along this high road you have good views of possible campsites along the creek. Near the end of the Pileup Creek bar a rough, unsigned trail climbs to the left. This is the route to Bruin Hill. The confluence of Kelly and Cayuse Creeks is a pretty spot with a nice camping area. Past there you commence a climb that takes you above the brush and into the forest, with occasional views of Kelly's Thumb ahead. A gentle descent brings you to Bear Creek Meadows and abundant campsites. From here you can continue up Kelly Creek to Hanson Meadows, two miles further.

You can also follow the Bear Creek Trail into Bear Creek Basin, taking the 26 mile Bruin Hill loop. After a half mile the Bear Creek Trail passes some campsites and fords the creek, as your USGS map shows. From 4300 to 4500 feet, the trail passes superb camping areas in lodgepole pine stands. You are still 2000 feet below the summit of Bruin Hill when you run out of basin and commence your climb. Fill your canteen when you leave the stream and start to switchback up the ridge. At a poorly signed "T" trail junction, turn left and continue to climb across open slopes. At the left end of a switchback, in trees that can shelter snow until July, cut left off the trail. Contour to the Little Moose Ridge Trail, which leads up to Bruin Hill. From the summit you can see craggy mountains, rounded ridges, and alluring valleys.

The Little Moose Trail descends to one saddle and continues on to the next, where it crosses a creek before traversing the ridge's north side. There are good campsites there. An outfitter camp marks the next saddle, from which you make the squiggly descent shown at the top of your Toboggan Ridge quadrangle. A trail cuts left to descend to another large camp with water, but you want to go right. After a descent you pass some springs where you should fill your canteens. Climb from here until the trail mysteriously divides. The left fork is a better trail that stays under the ridgetop and comes over its southwest finger just in time to descend past the head of Polar Creek. A descent brings you on to the Gorman Hill quad, where a stream provides the last water and campsites on the ridge. From the stream a series of ups and downs, punctuated by a delightful stretch of forest west of 5078, bring you to the trail divide between 4815 and 4705. Go left here and follow a switchback trail down, down, down to the Kelly Creek Trail.

Extensions: You could get lost by fording Kelly Creek to the Deer Creek or South, Middle, or North Fork Trails.

Access: Drive 41 miles east of Spalding Junction on US-12, to ID-11. Turn left, drive to Weippe, turn left there and drive to the French Mountain Road just south of Pierce. Turn right, and at ½ and 4¾ miles bear left. When the long descent down Orogrande Creek has ended, turn right and follow the North Fork Road to Kelly Creek Ranger Station. Go straight ahead on the Kelly Creek Road. At the Moose Creek Road junction, go straight to the trailhead, which is just before the Kelly Creek bridge. There is a campground back at the ranger station, and campsites after the first mile of trail.

At Bear Meadows

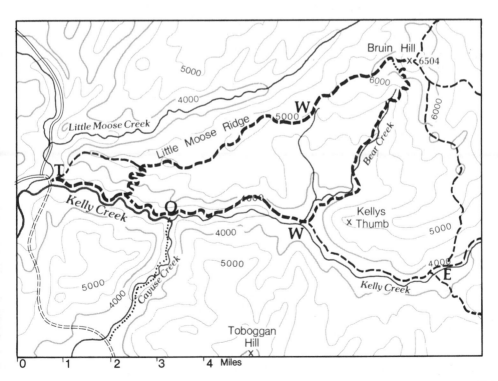

23. Windy Ridge

Hikes: D, O, W, E.
Total Distance, W: 12 miles.
Difficulty: Level II.
Season: July 10 — September 20.
Elevation Gain: 1200 feet.
USGS Map: Lookout Peak.
USFS Map: Clearwater N.F.
Mileage, Lew: 139 (12¼ dirt).

Introduction: This trail starts on the Lolo Motorway, which parallels Lewis and Clark's route of 1805 and 1806. Homage must be paid these first explorers of Idaho. As you drive on this low standard road and wonder if your car will make it, remember the day they travelled "28 miles over these mountains without relieving the horses from their packs or their having any food;" as you gripe about your freezedried dinner, remember Lewis' "portable soup", a dehydrated concoction that didn't even taste good to starving men; and as you speed along this maintained trail remember the party's difficult travels "over Steep points rocky & brushey" with an "emence quantity of falling timber." Today, the fate of this area hangs in the balance. The Monroe Butte, Lookout Peak and Cook Mountain area, the eastern anchor of the great Weitas Wilderness and the area with the greatest concentration of wolf sightings in Idaho, is being threatened by logging roads. The trail has a few rough and rocky spots that make it Level II.

The Trail: Weekenders can camp northeast of Monroe Butte, 6 miles in, or at Monroe Creek or Lake. Overnighters can make dry camps almost anywhere on the ridge, while dayhikers can reach the springs 3 miles in. The trail begins by climbing the ridge, and soon comes to broad lodgepole flats that mean dry camping. After you cross a long saddle you climb to the west side of 6422-6335 ridge, and just north of where your USGS map shows "Windy Ridge Camp" you come to a nice spring. At the next saddle a trail descends to the head of Mire Creek.

Past there you enter a world of trail junctions, all of which are signed. If you continue north on Windy Ridge, you cross a knoll at 6400, just east of Monroe Butte. You then descend on open ridge with good camping. Below and to the left is a pretty meadow. Water from the fork of Monroe Creek that rises in the meadow should be boiled. Monroe Lake, a big moose pond without fish, has campsites. It is reached by a rocky cross-country route. Turn right when the trail levels off from the descent off the 6400 knoll. Follow game trails to the rocky, non-treed areas shown in white on your USGS map. This rocky route is preferable to brushwhacking.

Extensions: All of the trails that branch off Windy Ridge offer high challenge. Most are ridgeline trails, with that to Lookout Mountain in good condition. There are small lakes near Lookout Mountain to supply water.

Access: Follow directions for Fish Creek (page 46), but continue 19½ miles further up US-12 to Saddle Camp Road. Turn left and drive 8¾ miles to the Lolo Motorway. Turn left on this little-maintained road, which has its share of rocks and ruts. Go 3½ miles to 12 Mile Saddle, where you can camp. Dry campsites come quickly on the trail.

A region of historic trails

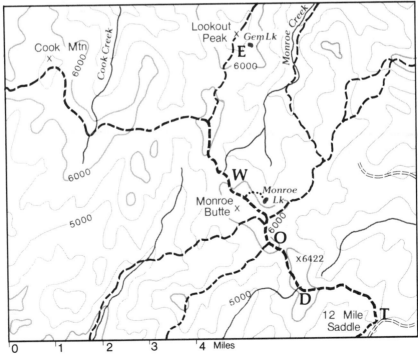

24. Mallard Larkins

Hikes: D, W, E.
Total Distance, W: 16 miles.
Difficulty: Levels I, III.
Season: July 1 – September 15.
Elevation Gain: 2300 feet.
USGS Maps: Buzzard Roost*,
  Mallard Peak.
USFS Map: Clearwater N. F.
USFS Pamphlet: Mallard Larkins
  Pioneer Area.
Mileage, Lew: 121 (12¾ dirt).

Introduction: The Mallard Larkins Pioneer Area embraces a high ridge extending from Larkins Peak east to Mallard Peak and then south to The Nub. This 30,500 acre area rises over 5000 feet above the North Fork of the Clearwater, and it has been severely glaciated. The ice left its mark in the rugged north side of the range, and some twenty lakes remain as a token of its presence. RARE-II recommended a 153,000 acre wilderness that includes the upper St Joe River. However, some 126,000 acres of contiguous roadless lands were left out. Whatever the fate of the larger area, the Pioneer Area will probably remain as wild and roadless as it is now. While the main ridge trail and most routes down to the lakes are Level I, the descent to Skyland Lake is Level III.

The Trail: Dayhikers can hike to Goat Ridge or Grassy Point, 2½ miles in. Overnighters will have problems, since Larkins Lake, 6 miles, has the first campsites with water. Weekenders can choose between Larkins Lake; Crag Lake, 7 miles; Heart Lake, 8 miles; Northbound Lake, 9 miles; or Skyland Lake, 11 miles. They all have campsites and character. The actual trailhead is not shown on the Buzzard Roost Quadrangle. It is in the southwest corner of Section 11, next to the "G" in "SMITH RIDGE". The trail now contours around the ridge's north side to reach 5388, instead of climbing over it. A considerable climb follows that brings you to Goat Ridge Peak, where you have an excellent view across Goat and Isabella Creeks toward Black Mountain and The Nub. From here on, the trail no longer follows the ridgeline but contours around the summits.

At the next saddle, you see the Elmer Creek Trail descend to the right. The next trail junction comes at 6391, where the Larkins Peak Trail climbs to the left. Go right, descend, and then climb to the Larkins Lake Trail junction. The ridge trail then contours to the Cataract Creek Trail, which leads to Crag Lake. You then hike on the southern flank of Crag Peak to reach Heart Pass. There are springs along the trail before and beyond this pass, where you leave the gentle southern exposure for the rocky northern slopes. You also get an overview of Heart Lake, to which a trail descends. Continuing east, you pass some possible campsites and a good stream. A trail leads to Northbound Lake, where there are many campsites.

The next saddle on the ridge trail is the takeoff point for the Martin Creek Trail, #479. And you might wish you had a flying machine to simplify the descent to Skyland Lake! When you meet your first stream at 5615, bear left. A few switchbacks bring you back to this stream later, but you again bear left. More switchbacks bring you to a long contouring stretch, which passes through brush, bogs, and boulders. There is no greener spot in all Idaho than the meadow below here – no place more reminiscent of Alaskan tundra. At last cross the creek, climb and descend, and at a blazed tree turn right and climb to Skyland Lake. Approach quietly, and you may surprise a bathing beauty named Minnie Moose.

Extensions: You could continue south to remote Black Mountain, east along Lost Ridge, or north to Fawn Lake.

Access: Drive 41 miles east of Spalding Junction on US-12, to ID-11. Turn left and follow it through Pierce to Headquarters. Once there, turn left and drive 24 miles on the paved Beaver Creek Road to the North Fork. Turn left on the Isabella Creek Road and follow it for 3¼ miles, then go left again and climb on the steep Smith Ridge Road. After 10 miles, in which you may encounter logging trucks, you come to the trailhead area, complete with outhouse. You could car camp in one of the campgrounds along the North Fork or dry camp along Goat Ridge, 2½ miles in.

Skyland Lake

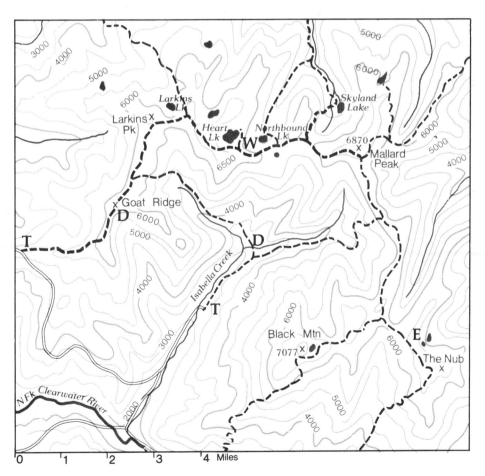

25. Moose Mountain

Hikes: D, O, W.
Total Distance, O: 10 miles.
Difficulty: Levels II, III.
Season: July 1—September 20.
Elevation Gain: 3400 feet.
USGS Map: Moose Mtn, Osier Ridge*.
USFS Map: Clearwater N.F.
Mileage, Lew: 135 (56½ dirt).

Introduction: The Moose Creek Buttes rank among Idaho's most scenic and rugged mountains. They were recommended for wilderness by RARE-II, and they have an inspirational value that makes them worthy of preservation. The cirques on the Buttes' north sides dazzle you with a three-tiered display of blue sky, tan rock, and green meadows. There are two access points to the area: from Deadwood Ridge to Moose Mountain the trail is Level II; from Moose Creek to Moose Mountain and south to the pond the trails are Level III. The Deadwood Ridge road is threatened with closure: check on its current condition at Kelly Creek Ranger Station.

The Trails: Dayhikers can go from Deadwood Ridge to Moose Mountain, 3 miles. Overnighters and weekenders must reach water, and the pond your map shows is a good source with good camping. The pond is 6 miles from Moose Creek, 5 miles from Deadwood Ridge. The Moose Creek Trail starts as a four wheel drive road. It bears right at a gate to private land, climbs to Deadwood Creek, crosses that creek, and then reaches Moose Creek, where it becomes a trail and doesn't cross. After a short walk on the trail you enter the Moose Mtn Quadrangle, and you then *do* cross the creek. Twice, in fact, as your map shows. There are many decent campsites in this level meadowed stretch. The USGS map continues to be accurate from here. There is no sure water after a creek at 4700 feet. Past there the trail worsens. There are good ridgeline campsites west of 5884 and 6135, where the trail improves again. Moose Mountain's summit, like so many others in this area, has the ruins of an old lookout. And what a view the lookouts had!

From Deadwood Ridge you climb through a perfect lodgepole forest, with campsites on the ridge to the right. At 5400 feet you come to water, and shortly after you meet Trail 427. Turn left, pass a nice spur on your left (where you could camp), cross the saddle at 5617, and climb to the top. While the trail is rocky, it is never really steep. The trail divide below Moose Mountain is hard to locate, and the trail south of here is hard to follow—but fun to play cat and mouse with. There is indeed a trail of sorts down to the pond east of 6745. It leaves by a big blazed tree, and initially descends at a moderate pace. Only at the last does it show its true colors and make a headlong plunge to the pond. There are many campsites here, with more in the meadow a bit farther south.

Extension: Probably a mere handful of people climb the Moose Creek Buttes each year.

Access: Follow directions for Kelly Creek, but turn north on the Pierce-Superior Road. After 3½ miles turn left and ford Moose Creek. Drive ½ mile and bear right; then after ½ mile more there is a small meadow to the left where you can pull over and park. The gate/4WD road junction where the route goes right is a short ½ mile from here, but there is no parking there. Campsites are on Moose Creek by the road and trail. To reach the Deadwood Ridge Trail drive 8¼ miles up from Kelly Creek, over Deception Saddle to Road 734. After 1½ miles bear left; after 1¼ miles bear left again, and the trailhead is 1¾ miles further. In 1981 the wrong trail's sign was at the trailhead! No camping is along this road, but there are campsites just up the trail.

The Moose Buttes

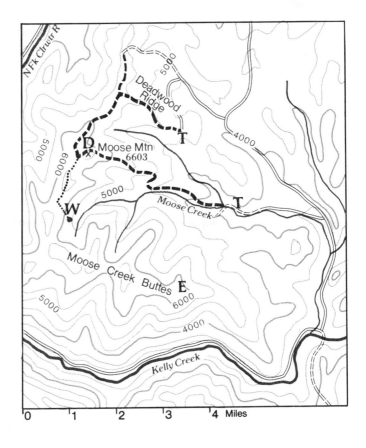

26. Pot Mountain

Hikes: D, O, W, E.
Total Distance, W: 18 miles.
Difficulty: Level II.
Season: July 4 – September 20.
Elevation Gain: 4700 feet.
USGS Maps: Pot Mountain, The Nub*.
USFS Map: Clearwater N.F.
Other Source: *Early Days in the Forest Service, Volume 4;* by USFS.
Mileage, Lew: 128 (50 dirt).

Introduction: Pot is one of the legendary mountains of the Clearwater country. At 7139, it provides the finest panorama of North Central Idaho. This great mass of granite forces the river below to make a radical detour to the south. At present there are no roads south of upper Quartz Creek, and the Pot Mountain area is pure wilderness (except for the activities of helicopter loggers). The Forest Service, however, believes it can successfully road and log the region, a belief the author questions. The trails on Pot Mountain are in surprisingly good condition, considering their steep pitch. Due to the occasional 40 percent grades, they are rated Level II.

The Trail: You could day or overnight hike to the top of Pot Mountain, 3 miles in and 2400 feet up. The Buckingham Lake area, 9 miles in, beckons to weekenders. The trail begins as a road through a clearcut. From 4793 climb on the road, round a corner to the right, and at the end of the short straight-away bear left on a closed-off road. (The "good" road here goes right and then along the north side of the ridge to reach an atrocious clearcut.) Your closed-off road, the one shown on The Nub map, stays in this drainage and after 15 minutes divides. Go left, cross the creek, then go right. Continue straight ahead to the ridgeline. The route now climbs directly up the ridge to the left, on a ditched out road.

It soon becomes trail, and *steep*. Note how the trunks of the hemlocks are bent from rapid soil movement. At about 5800 feet there is a divide. One trail goes left and down to an eerie springs, near which you could camp. The main trail bears right and mellows out a bit. Where it traverses the

mountain's right flank the author saw a big doe apparently chasing a coyote. Were there fawns nearby? The trail meets the ridge about 150 feet below the summit. It cuts right, passing possible campsites, and comes to a clearing with a helispot. To the left, here, a very old trail descends to water (except in the driest years – if you can't see water below, don't make the effort). A real highlight of your view is the small but perfect cirque below Bar Point.

Continuing north, you descend to the Bar Point Trail. The saddle at 6204 is next, followed by the climb your map shows to the ridgeline west of 6638. The grassy saddle above the trail there is one of Idaho's most sublime points. Another descent takes you to the Squaw Creek Trail divide, at a saddle where you can camp. Twenty minutes further there is water, and an equal time brings you to a meadow where you can camp. Buckingham Lake, a big shallow pond, has some campsites on a hill to the north.

Extensions: A week could easily be spent exploring this wilderness, whose highlights are the soaring rock outcrops near Buckingham Point, the cirque southeast of Pot Mountain, and the Bar Point area.

Access: Follow directions for Kelly Creek (page 62) as far as the North Fork Clearwater Road. Turn right here and after 16 miles, turn left on the Mush Saddle Road. After 8½ miles you pass the saddle, where you can camp. After another 1½ miles turn left at Mush Point. Turn right after ½ mile, and after ¾ mile go left, cross Quartz Creek, and drive ¼ mile to the first switchback (4793), where there is room to park. The road is four wheel drive from here on. First campsites on the trail are at a logged saddle, one mile in.

The view southeast of Pot

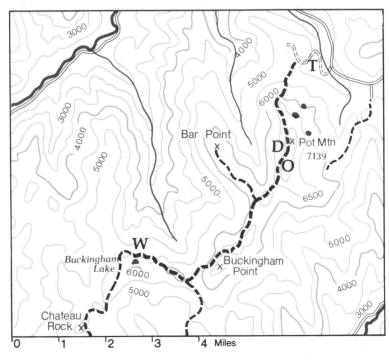

27. Goose Lake Loop

Hikes: D, O, W, E.
Total Distance, W: 25 miles.
Difficulty: Levels I, III.
Season: July 4 – September 20.
Elevation Gain: 4600 feet.
USGS Map: Straight Peak (1:62,500).
USFS Map: Clearwater N.F.
Mileage, Lew: 153 (73½ dirt);
    CdA, 153 (37 dirt).

Introduction: This area along the Idaho-Montana state divide, rich in miner and Indian history, is part of the proposed Big Burn Wilderness. It is high, open, grassy country (with a few rocks, too). There are routefinding problems once you leave the trails that lead to Goose and Fish Lakes, and follow the State Divide Trail: Level I on the way to the lakes, Level III in between.
The Trail: The loop hike to Goose Lake, then to Fish Lake via the State Divide Trail, and finally back via Lake Creek, is a strenuous weekend hike, 25 miles long. Overnighters and dayhikers can hike to the Goose Creek meadows, 4 miles in, or to Goose Lake, 5 miles. Most of the five mile route to Fish Lake is an old road, which was excluded from the proposed wilderness. It may be reopened for access to timber on private lands. The Goose Lake trail has some confusing points in the early going. After five minutes of hiking bear left on an older logging road. A mile later, when you come to a campsite, the trail begins on your right. As you cross the 5000 foot level, grassy slopes across the creek open the view up to 6780; a sign points out Goose Creek Falls; and you come to Steep Creek. After a stiff climb take the switchback to the right, and soon after, when you meet the Steep Lakes Trail, bear left. The Goose Creek meadows, where you can camp, are just ahead. Perhaps you will spy an eagle working this meadow, flying wingtip to grasstop, preying for a rodent errant. At the end of the meadow the trail climbs abruptly to the right and detours through the meadow due west of 6670. Turn left when you meet the stream that drains it. This is the last good water for 9 miles. Goose Lake is not far, a shallow fishless

affair with camping.

The easy hiking ends here! The trail that leads south along the divide goes straight up the ridge from the trail sign. It contours to a saddle and turns right. Once on the ridgetop follow the trail when you can see it and your instincts when you can't. The hiking varies from steep and rocky to smooth and grassy. There are meadows and ponds to the east, and possible campsites on the ridge. And best of all, there is the view of Steep Lakes. Here the Bitterroot Divide has made a rare bend to the east, and glaciers have carved one of the most scenic basins in Idaho. You can reach the upper lake from the mini-saddle past Milepost 204.211. The steepest climb of the loop follows, but past here the trail becomes more gentle, with abundant ridgeline campsites. You can camp at Upper Siamese Lake, but access is difficult. A trail starts the descent from the saddle, but it vanishes halfway down.

As you continue south on the main trail, you overlook one lake and then descend via switchbacks to the level of the small lake below 7075, where you can camp. The trail junction above Fish Lake, where you turn right, is well marked. There is good water in the meadow west of the lake, and camping in the woods nearby. There are no campsites on the old road down Fish Creek.
Extensions: You could go farther north or south on the State Divide Trail, or hike a side trail into Montana.
Access: Follow directions for Moose Mountain (page 68), but go straight over Deception Summit to the North Fork. Turn right and drive 3½ miles to the Fish Lake Creek Road, and turn right again. At the divide 5 miles in, bear left for the Goose Lake Trail, or right for the Fish Lake Trail. Campsites come soon on the former trail, and five miles in on the latter. You can car camp at the Cedars Campground. To reach the area from Coeur d'Alene, take I-90 east to Superior, MT, and turn off at Exit 47. Go through the big lumber mill and over Hoodoo Pass, turning left 11 miles beyond the pass.

Steep Lakes cirque

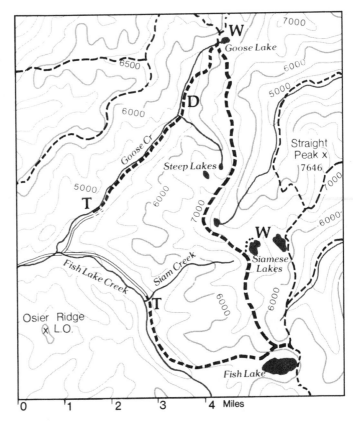

28. To the Lost Lakes

Hikes: D, O, W, E.
Total Distance, W: 15 miles.
Difficulty: Levels I, III.
Season: July 15 — September 20.
Elevation Gain: 2800 feet.
USGS Maps: Cayuse Junction,
   Rhodes Peak.
USFS Map: Clearwater N.F.
Mileage, Lew: 170 (21¼ dirt).

Introduction: Cayuse Creek is one of Idaho's most remarkable streams. The name Lost Lakes is very apt for it source, since the creek seems quite lost. It flows southwest, west, northwest, and finally northeast before reaching Kelly Creek. High above Lost Lakes are peaks that reach 7930 feet. Like upper Cayuse Creek, they are part of the proposed Big Burn Wilderness. The trail to Lost Lakes is easy to follow and to walk, Level I; the loop via Williams Lake is difficult, steep, and in part untrailed, Level III.

The Trail: Dayhikers can enjoy either the Silver Creek or Cayuse Creek Trails; overnighters can reach Lost Lakes, 4½ miles; weekenders can take the 15 mile loop. The loop route follows the Cayuse Creek Trail to the junction at 5167 and turns north up Silver Creek. This is a good trail as far as the Silver Creek crossing, just below the confluence with Billy Rhodes Creek, where you can camp. The trail climbs nicely until you reach 5726, where it tries to disappear on the open ridge. There are faint switchbacks there, and the trail can't "lose" you: just keep going up the ridge and you'll meet it again. The junction with the trail from Blacklead Mountain is not signed. Add a rock to the cairn, turn right, and move under some extraordinary cirques well worth exploring. The one before Goat Lake offers cold water and decent camping, as does Goat Lake. The trail reappears across the Goat Lake outlet creek, climbs to some bad water, and then begins a surprisingly gentle climb to Williams Peak. There is camping by the lakes at 7005 and 6647. The loop route goes south from 7429. It descends a rocky slope to the saddle east of 7466, climbs up on the ridge, and meets a good horse trail that goes down to 7146 and to the saddle with 6793 (watch for 6592, a good landmark to the east). From the saddle you can cross-country to the Lost Lakes over open forest slopes with a few downed trees. You can camp in the lodgepoles north of the middle lake.

The only problem with the Cayuse Creek Trail to Lost Lakes is the unsigned trail divide west of the lakes. When you leave the lakes, take the trail that bears to the north, and descends to Cayuse Creek via a side creek. There are a few campsites on the trail at about 5400 feet. The few up-down stretches of trail serve the useful function of allowing you to stay on one side of Cayuse Creek.

Extensions: You could continue past the Williams Lakes to the Idaho-Montana Divide. You can also hike *down* Cayuse Creek.

Access: Drive 156 miles east of Spalding Junction on US-12 to Road 569, the Parachute Hill Road. After 2½ miles, bear left. When you meet Road 500, turn left and follow it to Cayuse Junction. Turn right and drive 1½ miles to the unsigned trailhead. There are campsites on the road, and just down the trail.

Looking across Silver Creek

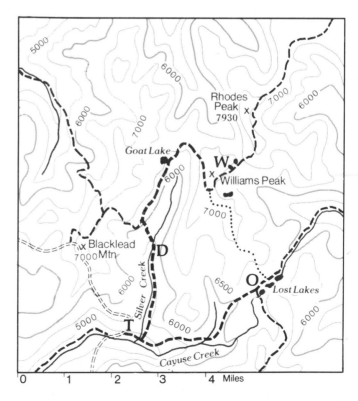

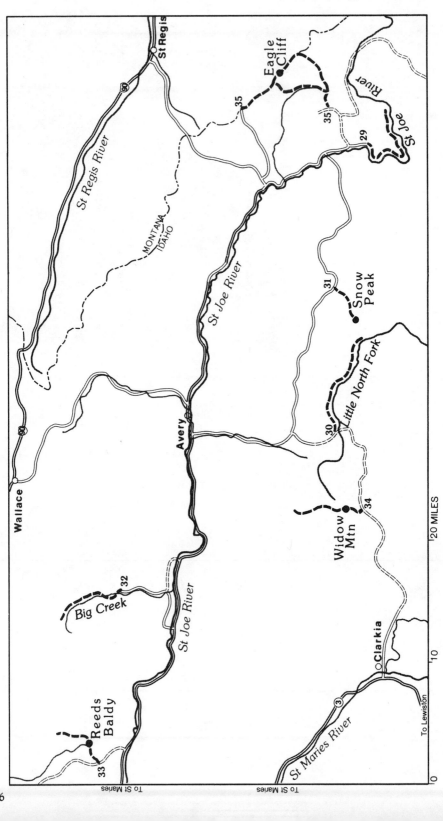

St Regis

St Regis River

MONTANA
IDAHO

Eagle
Cliff

35

35

29

St Joe River

St Joe River

Snow
Peak

31

Little North Fork

30

Wallace

Avery

Widow
Mtn

34

Big Creek

32

St Joe River

Clarkia

Reeds
Baldy

33

St Maries River

To Lewiston

3

To St Maries

To St Maries

0

10

20 MILES

On and Off the St Joe

The St Joe River drains several excellent backcountry hiking areas. Unfortunately, the quantity of St Joe roadless area is due to decline: of ten roadless areas identified by RARE-II, only Mallard Larkins was recommended for wilderness. Most of the rejected areas have problems unique to the St Joe region. Many suffer from fragmented land ownership, for much of the region has railroad-grant sections alternating with Forest Service land in a checkerboard array. There are also State of Idaho and Bureau of Land Management inholdings. Several areas are finally recovering from the devastating fires of 1910. Some 70 firefighters perished in the St Joe drainage on August 20 and 21, 1910. Brush is at last yielding to trees, and timber harvest is now becoming economic. Still other areas are severely impacted by roads, and really too small for effective wilderness management. A major issue is the use of chemical defoliants to clear brush for tree planting.

The Forest Service has an excellent opportunity to "show its stuff" here. It can develop the nine roadless areas in a responsible and imaginative fashion, preserving dispersed recreation, wildlife, and watershed values. It can leave significant areas like Bronson Meadows, Nelson Peak, and Eagle Cliff in their *de facto* wilderness state. Or, it can bulldoze through plans and roads without regard for any values but Timber. A good start has been made with the State Divide Trail, now a National Recreation Trail; and with the promotion of the Nelson Peak trail system. Please keep up the good work!

29. The Upper St Joe

Hikes: D, O, W, E.
Total Distance, W: 18 miles.
Difficulty: Level I.
Season: May 1—September 20.
Elevation Gain: 800 feet.
USGS Maps: Bacon Peak,
  Simmons Peak (1:62,500).
USFS Map: St Joe N.F.; or I.P.N.F.
Mileage, CdA: 134 (24½ dirt);
  Lew, 200 (34 dirt).

Introduction: This is a popular trail, highly esteemed for its beautiful river and mountain scenery, its many fine campsites, and the quality fishing it accesses. It was endorsed by the USFS for inclusion in the proposed Mallard Larkins Wilderness. It is a vital addition to that backcountry area, for this trail provides both access to the river corridor in early season and access to the Bacon Peak—Five Lakes Butte—Lost Ridge high country in the summer. This is a good trail, easy to follow: Level I.

The Trail: Weekenders can stop 8 or 9 miles in, at Mile 114 Bar or Broken Leg Creek. Dayhikers and overnighters have many choices starting 2½ miles in, at Timber Creek. The trailhead at the end of Spruce Tree Campground is well signed. The initial stretch to Timber Creek follows an old road and offers classic views of the meandering river below. At Timber Creek the trail becomes two: a foot trail always on the north side, and a horse trail that crosses and recrosses the river with abandon. There is good camping at the last two bars shown on your Simmons Peak map (level white areas free of green woodland overprint). From here to the bar just past St Joe Lodge (the cabin square shown on the Bacon Peak Quadrangle), there is no camping. Past there, campsites come often. Once you

have rounded the bend at Ruby Creek, you begin a series of climbs and descents which are punctuated by views of the Bacon Peak-Five Lakes Butte high country. A final climb via switchbacks above a spot where the river has reclaimed the trail brings you to the Broken Leg Creek flats, nine miles in. This is a suitable distance and site for an early season camp.

Extensions: The St Joe can usually be forded in early July, and you can then hike up Bacon, Bean, Ruby or Pass Creeks to the beckoning mountains, or use the horse trail (which peters out at Mile 112¼). You could also continue another 9 miles along the river, to the Heller Creek trailhead.

Access: From Coeur d'Alene, drive 97 miles east on I-90 until you are 1 mile west of St. Regis, Montana. Turn right on the Little Joe Road. Drive over the divide down to the St Joe River Road and turn left. The road to Red Ives has now been improved. Take the river road past the ranger station to Spruce Tree Campground. Camp there or on the trail below the Elbow Ridge Trail sign, about 1½ miles in. From Lewiston, go east on US-12, then turn left on ID-3 and follow it to St. Maries, where you turn right on the St Joe River Road. Gold Creek and the road to Red Ives, where you bear right, is 74 miles upriver.

Magnificent meanders

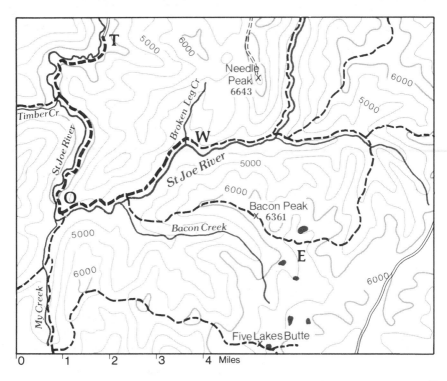

30. The Little North Fork

Hikes: D, O, W, E.
Total Distance, W: 16 miles.
Difficulty: Levels I, II.
Season: May 1—September 20.
Elevation Gain: 700 feet.
USGS Maps: Monumental Butte,
  Montana Peak.
USFS Maps: St Joe N.F.; or I.P.N.F.
Mileage, CdA: 116 (27 dirt);
  Lew: 152 (27 dirt).

Introduction: The Little North Fork
Clearwater River has a fine trail that offers
good early season hiking and good later
season access to wilderness. If you can
overlook the occasional messes left by
trailbikers, you will enjoy hiking along this
magnificent stream. Level I as far as the
ford at Spotted Louis Creek, Level II
beyond.
The Trail: Overnighters and weekenders
can choose from numerous campsites along
the trail to Spotted Louis, 8 miles in.
Dayhikers can just walk until they find a
pool or falls to sit and contemplate. Once
on the trail you soon come to Twin Creek,
and from here to Rutledge Creek there are
many campsites. Better sites come in cedars
a bit farther, from 3300 to 3200 feet. There
are many campsites and an old cabin
around Montana Creek, and a small
camping area across the challenging ford of
Spotted Louis Creek.
Extensions: You could continue down the
Little North Fork to the Snow Peak Trail (8
miles), or to the Canyon, Larkins, or Foehl
Creek Trails (15, 16, 17 miles). All these
trails climb to high, wild country.
Access: Drive to St. Maries and go 43 miles
up the St Joe River Road. Turn right on the
Fishhook Creek Road 301 and follow it for
12¼ miles, to the big intersection with
Road 216 (just east of Fortynine Meadows
on your USGS map). Turn left and descend
along Adair Creek to the road that goes left
just before you reach the Adair Creek
bridge. The trailhead is a mile down this
road, near the corner of Sections 11, 12, 13,
and 14. Camp there or 1½ miles down the
trail.

31. Snow Peak

Hikes: D, O.
Total Distance, O: 10 miles.
Difficulty: Level II.
Season: July 4—September 20.
Elevation Gain: 2600 feet.
USGS Maps: Bathtub Mtn,
  Montana Peak.
USFS Map: St Joe N.F.; or, I.P.N.F.
Mileage, CdA: 134 (44 dirt);
  Lew: 170 (44 dirt).

Introduction: Snow Peak is one of north
Idaho's most striking mountains. Rising
4000 feet above the Little North Fork, its
upper slopes are almost sheer rock cliffs.
The local mountain goat herd has reacted
poorly to noise, and the trail is open only to
foot and horse travel; please don't be noisy
or harass the goats. The trail is occasionally
rough and rocky, but always easy to
follow: Level II.
The Trail: Snow Peak is 5 miles in, a tough
dayhike. The camping area below it, 4½
miles in, makes a good overnighter's goal.
The trail starts by climbing straight up the
ridgeline to a level area between the two
6316's. It then descends to a saddle at 5500,
where you can see all the soil that has
washed down the trail. Continue on the
obvious trail. After climbing about 350
feet, where the main trail cuts right, you see
an inviting meadow and a soaring peak.
There is camping to the left, climbing to the
right. The uphill to the lookout is steep and
rocky, but the junction at 6230, where you
turn left, is signed. And the summit is hard
to miss!
Extensions: You could hike 4½ miles down
the Spotted Louis Trail to the Little North
Fork.
Access: Follow the directions above to the
Fishhook Creek Road, where you also turn
right. Drive 9¾ miles to Road 201 and turn
left. Follow this road 26½ miles to the
trailhead, keeping a very good watch for
logging trucks. There is a campground at
Mammouth Springs (just north of Dismal
Lake), and limited camping in the trailhead
area. First campsites on the trail are dry
ones ½ mile in.

One special spot

Mountain goat country

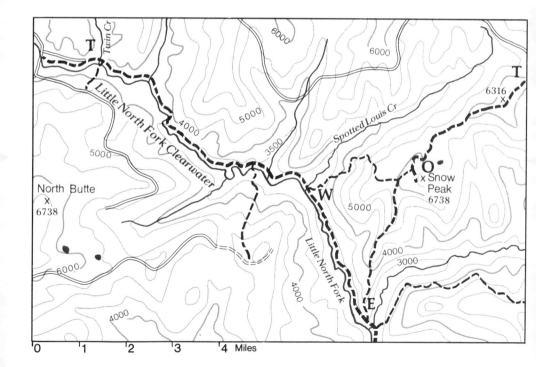

32. Big Creek Backcountry

Hikes: D, O, W.
Total Distance, O: 8 miles.
Difficulty: Levels I, II.
Season: May 1 – September 20.
Elevation Gain: 900 feet.
USGS Map: Calder (1:62,500).
USFS Map: St Joe N.F.; or, I.P.N.F.
Mileage, CdA: 56½ (14¾ dirt);
   Lew: 126½ (12¾ dirt).

Introduction: Bronson Meadows, where ten firefighters perished on August 20, 1910, is in the center of an area which has been little disturbed since that awful day. It is south of the divide between the St Joe and Coeur d'Alene Rivers, a divide known by the USGS as the St Joe Mountains, by the USFS as the Coeur d'Alene Divide. To add to the confusion in the area, this is also the divide between Big Creek and Big Creek, two major creeks that flow into two rivers! Bronson Meadows is huge, 2 miles wide in spots. And Bronson Meadows is eerie, for the spirits of the dead firefighters still inhabit the area. Two hikes are described here: one up the Middle Fork Big Creek to Bronson Meadows, Level II; and one along the divide from Elsie Lake, Level I.

The Trails: Bronson Meadows is only 3½ miles in, but three stream crossings make the trail seem longer. You start by quickly climbing 400 feet, only to descend to the first ford. This one could be tough, and it shouldn't be tried during high water. Beyond here the canyon widens, and the two remaining fords are much easier. Bronson Meadows offers abundant campsites. Jump across the Middle Fork above its confluence with Ames/Early Creek, and watch for a trail divide. To the right, Trail 155 climbs the hill on its way to the Coeur d'Alene Divide. To the left, Trail 44 continues up to Kellogg Saddle, starting on the creek's east side (not the left, as your map shows). There are numerous wet stretches, creek crossings, brushy interludes, and beaver pond sightings on

the way up.

The area can also be approached from Elsie Lake. While much of what the Forest Service calls "trail" in this area is really four wheel drive road, with heavy motorcycle traffic, there are some scenic views and decent dayhikes here. Take the road to the right of the Elsie Lake outhouse that parallels a small stream. After a right turn, cross the stream and begin to climb on the trail. Pass over a very nice ridge (worth exploring), descend to a small lake, and climb to a saddle. Turn right at the trail divide, then go left and traverse the south side of the ridge. Stretches of good trail still parallel the road as far as 5961, which gives a good view of Bronson Meadows and Pond Creek. You can loop back to Elsie Lake via a closed road that descends to the main road.

Access: For Elsie Lake, drive east on I-90 from Coeur d'Alene Junction to Exit 54, Big Creek. Drive through the Sunshine Mine area and then climb on the narrow and steep, yet relatively smooth road. When you reach Elsie Lake, turn left to the outhouse/camping area. For Bronson Meadows, drive to St. Maries via I-90 and ID-3 (or US-12 and ID-3, from Spalding). Take the St Joe River Road and drive 23½ miles to the Calder Road, where you turn left. Turn right in town on the North Side Road, then drive 5¼ miles to the Big Creek Road. Turn left and drive to its end. There is a Forest Service campground on the road, and camping 3 miles in.

Bronson Meadows

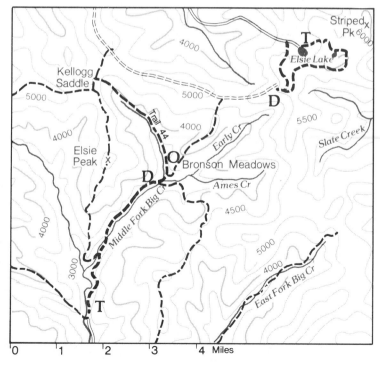

33. Over Reeds Baldy

Hikes: D, O.
Total Distance, O: 12 miles.
Difficulty: Levels I, III.
Season: June 25 — September 20.
Elevation Gain: 1100 feet.
USGS Map: St Joe (1:62,500).
USFS Map: St Joe N.F.; or I.P.N.F.
Mileage, CdA: 50 (20¾ dirt).

Introduction: The western end of the Coeur d'Alene Divide is anchored by a high ridge that runs from north to south. Poised to intercept severe weather from the Pacific, with their vegetation stunted and wind-shaped, St Joe Baldy (5825), Reeds Baldy (6153), Latour Peak (6408), and Latour Baldy (6232) are the major summits on the ridge. This land is managed by the BLM, not the Forest Service, and it has been studied as a potential wilderness. Two trails cross the area: an easy, popular, Level I trail to Crystal Lake; and a challenging old Level III trail/route over Reeds Baldy.

The Trail: Crystal Lake and Reeds Baldy are 2 and 2½ mile dayhikes. There are good dry campsites around 6080 and 6168, about 6 miles in, for overnight hikers. A lack of water makes long trips impractical. Start on an old jeep road that climbs the ridge for a way. The trail you want is an excellent wide one, unsigned but obvious, that cuts off the road to the right. It contours and then makes a shaded descent to the saddle between Pearson and Reeds Baldy. This good trail climbs a bit and then descends to beautiful Crystal Lake. A camping area at the north side of the lake is marked by several iron cooking grates. Unfortunately, there is no firewood left in the area! The small, trampled, littered camping area leads the author to recommend against camping at the lake.

The author bushwhacked from the lake to the ridge near 5960. The ridge trail has probably never been a very good one; at present, it is very poor and generally hard to follow. But it has a unique character you'll enjoy getting acquainted with. And it *will* challenge you! It is non-signed and non-existent where it leaves the Crystal Lake Trail at the saddle. It seems to stay close to the cirque-side of the ridge until it leaves the forest. When it enters the rock realm, which lasts as far as the old fire road south of 6063, it follows the ridgeline, dropping off the side occasionally where darker rocks mark a path. Climb to the top of 6063, and beyond it in the forest you will find good dry campsites and a better trail. Bear to the left as you climb from the saddle past 6080, and there is a serene meadow well suited to dry camping. The pond your map shows northwest of 6168 dries up in late summer.

Extensions: None, unless you wish to tackle the maze of roads and trails along the divide to the east.

Access: From Coeur d'Alene Junction, drive 28 miles east on I-90 to Cataldo Exit 40. Turn south (left) on the Latour Creek/Rochat Divide Road. Although there are many road junctions along the way, your road is always the best one, and it is usually signed. At 16¾ miles from the highway, bear left. The trailhead is at a road divide 4 miles beyond. There is some camping at a springs south of Rochat Peak, on the road. The first sites on the trail are dry ones on the saddle above Crystal Lake. You can also reach the trailhead by way of a very poor road from the St Joe River Road, 11½ miles from ID-3.

Crystal Lake

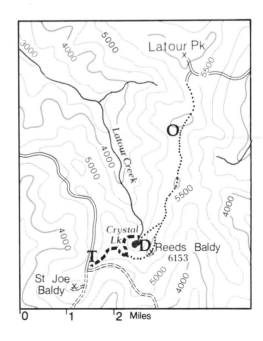

34. Widow Mountain

Hikes: D, O.
Total Distance, O: 11 miles.
Difficulty: Levels I, II.
Season: July 4 – September 20.
Elevation Gain: 3000 feet.
USGS Map: Widow Mtn.
USFS Map: Clearwater N. F.; or
  St. Joe N. F.
Mileage, CdA: 107 (21 dirt);
  Lew: 81 (21 dirt).

Introduction: North of Dworshak Reservoir a high country area stops many storms and starts many streams, including the Little North Fork Clearwater River and Marble Creek. This area is a curiosity: a timbered alpine region managed by the BLM, which is studying it as a possible wilderness. (Most BLM land in Idaho is better known for sagebrush than for hemlock.) The western part of this high area is dominated by Grandmother and Grandfather Mountains. The eastern part, described here, is capped by Widow Mountain (6828), which enjoys a panoramic view of north central Idaho. The route follows a good, Level I trail except for a rocky, Level II stretch over Lookout Mountain and a trailless descent to Fish Lake.

The Trail: Dayhikers can reach Widow Mountain, 1½ miles in, or Lookout Peak, 3½ miles in. Overnighters can camp on the ridge or at Fish Lake, 5½ miles in. The trail now starts at 5922, the saddle just northwest of Orphan Point. It generally climbs along the ridgeline and stays in the trees until it cuts north to contour along the east side of 6582. There are some dry but scenic campsites along the ridge here. As you descend along the west side of Widow Mountain, you meet the old Widow Mountain-Fortynine Meadows Trail. This trail is so old it just isn't there anymore! To reach Widow Mountain, just climb up the ridge. The summit is distinguished by more than its view: along its north side rocks spell out W-I-D-O-W M-T. A final attrac-

tion is the perfect meadow to the east of the peak.

Back on the trail to Fish Lake, you come to lush meadows, possible campsites, and cool water. The trail then cuts right and descends to the saddle above Lost Lake. There, a sign grimly warns you against attempting the descent to the lake, which has taken two lives. But there are good campsites here, with views of sunrise, sunset, and lake.

From the saddle the trail climbs a bit, bears right at a mystery junction, and climbs a lot more, up to the rocky summit of Lookout Mountain. It continues north along and to the right of the ridgeline. Suddenly, miraculously, you meet a new improved version of the trail shown on your USGS map. It switchbacks down to the Fish Lake saddle, and up to the trailhead at Breezy Point. The descent to Fish Lake is certainly easier than that to Lost Lake. There are a few campsites down at the lake and many up on the saddle.

Access: Drive to Clarkia on ID-3, from either I-90 and Rose Lake, or US-12 and Kendrick. Turn into town, go right on the paved road, and just past the schoolhouse turn left. After 1 mile turn right, and after 4½ more miles, at Gold Center, turn left and start the bumpy climb to the high country. Stay on Road 301 for 15½ miles. The trailhead is a poor road to the left. There are many roadside campsites in the area. The first sites on the trail are dry ones ¾ miles in.

Rainy day ridgeline camping

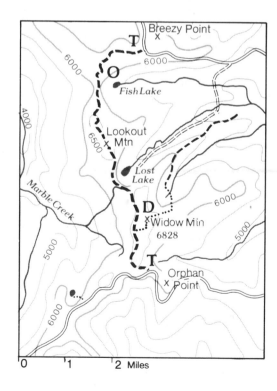

35. Eagle Cliff

Hikes: D, O, W, E.
Total Distance, W: 18 miles.
Difficulty: Levels II, III.
Season: July 1 – September 20.
Elevation Gain: 3500 feet.
USGS Maps: Illinois Peak,
  Simmons Peak* (both 1:62,500).
USFS Map: St Joe N. F.; or,
  I. P. N. F.
Mileage, CdA: 143 (36 dirt);
  Lew, 189 (36 dirt).

Introduction: East of Red Ives Ranger Station the State Divide Trail offers exciting hiking, passing over peaks like Eagle Cliff that tower above lakes and valleys. The scenics and silences here are marred at times by the sights and sounds of logging in Simmons Creek, but the pleasures of the area's high trails far outweigh the pains of those low roads. The Divide Trail is Level II, rocky with a few tricky spots, but the Simmons Creek part of the loop is Level III, with routefinding problems.

The Trails: There are two trailheads for the area, Little Joe and Simmons Ridge. From the former, dayhikers can climb 3 miles to Eagle Cliff; overnighters can hike 2½ or 3 miles to Washout Springs or Cliff Lake; and weekenders can hike 6 or 7 miles to Idaho or Heart Lakes. From Simmons Ridge, dayhikers can go 3 miles to viewpoints along the Simmons-Heller Trail; overnighters can go 3 or 5 miles to Simmons Creek or Idaho Lake; and weekenders can hike a tough 18 mile loop along the State Divide, Washout, and Simmons Creek Trails. From Little Joe Mountain, the trail starts by climbing a peak at 6900 feet. It then descends to a saddle and the Washout Trail junction, which is unsigned but well blazed. Campsites and water are just down this trail. You meet the Cliff Lake Trail soon after. It quickly goes down to the lake, where there is camping. On the main route a switchbacking trail takes you almost to the summit of Eagle Cliff, a most noble peak. As you descend off the mountain you can see Idaho Lake, where you can camp. It is easily accessible from the saddle below.

The loop hike from Simmons Ridge begins with a dry 5 mile hike to the State Divide. After the first 1½ miles you meet the Simmons Creek Trail, unsigned but obvious. Stay to the left as you cross the bald knob at 6780, and on the saddle just beyond, a faint but easy-to-follow trail bears left. It contours serenely along the ridge until it precipitously drops to Idaho Lake. The main trail embarassingly disappears just before meeting the State Divide Trail. That trail is easy to find, though, and you can follow it south to Heart Lake or north along the loop. Going north, you descend to the saddle from which leaves the more sensible route to Idaho Lake. Climb over Eagle Cliff, and when you reach the first saddle past 7007, go left on the Washout Trail. Its long, gradual descent ends at an extraordinarily steep downhill stretch, which would be hazardous in wet weather. At its conclusion you are at the confluence of three streams. You can camp here. Cross the little creek to your right, follow the trail to a sign on a post in a clearing, then go left and recross the creek. Once on the other side, turn right and cross Simmons Creek. Turn left and climb. This trail follows the west side of Simmons Creek, not the east side as your USGS map shows. Don't be fooled when you cross Goat Creek: continue straight ahead after crossing. Once at the ridge trail, turn right for car and home!

Extensions: The State Divide Trail, now a National Recreation Trail, extends all the way south to Granite Pass.

Access: Follow directions for the St Joe River Trail (page 78) to the St Joe-Gold Creek Road junction. To reach Little Joe, go 1¾ miles back up Gold Creek to its East Fork Road, and turn right. After 4½ miles go straight. Bear left at a "T" intersection after 6¼ more miles. The trailhead is 3¾ miles away, right at the divide. You can car camp along the St Joe or dry camp on the ridge trail. Start with a full canteen. To reach the Simmons-Heller Trail, drive just past Red Ives Ranger Station to the Red Ives Creek Road. Drive 9¼ steep, rocky miles to the Simmons Ridge Road. Turn left and go ½ mile to the trailhead. You can camp there or on the dry ridge trail after 3 miles.

Binocular Peak

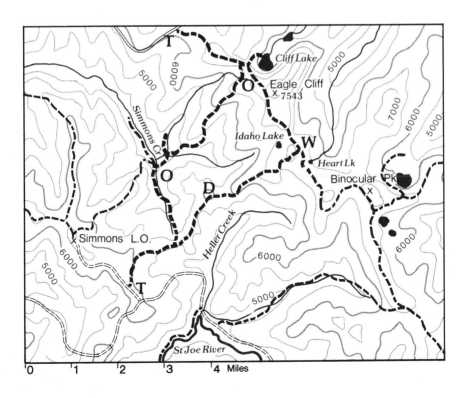

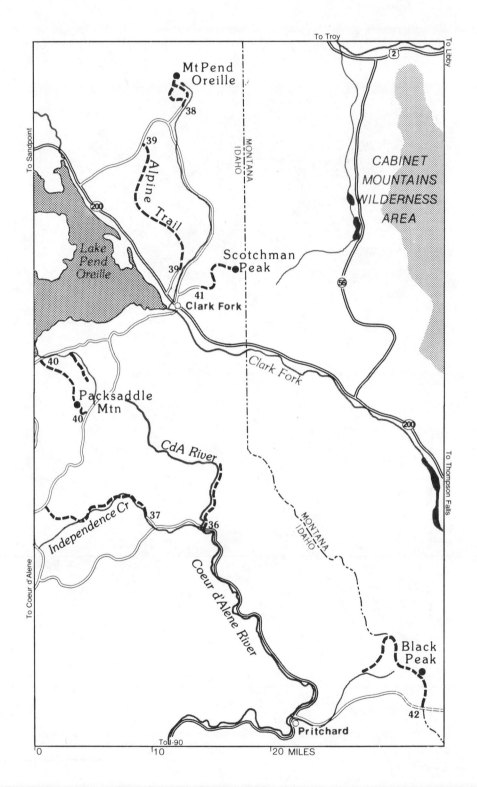

To Troy

To Libby

2

CABINET
MOUNTAINS
WILDERNESS
AREA

To Sandpoint

Mt Pend
Oreille

38

39

Alpine Trail

200

MONTANA
IDAHO

39

Scotchman
Peak

56

Lake
Pend
Oreille

39

41

Clark Fork

40

Clark Fork

40

Packsaddle
Mtn

200

To Thompson Falls

CdA River

Independence Cr

37

36

Coeur d'Alene River

MONTANA
IDAHO

To Coeur d'Alene

Black
Peak

42

Toll-90

Pritchard

0   10   20 MILES

Coeur d'Alene and Clark Fork

The Coeur d'Alene River marks the southern boundary of the Idaho Panhandle, while the Clark Fork River marks the northern limit of the Bitterroot Divide. The part of Idaho drained by these two streams provides a classic illustration of vanishing wilderness. One need only glance from the Mt. Pend Oreille Quadrangle (1951) to the Idaho Panhandle National Forest Travel Plan (1974) to see the change. A more detailed examination reveals that in 1951 there were about 18 miles of road on the map. At present there are at least 140 miles of road. This situation has been duplicated throughout the area: the Packsaddle Mountain, Burke, Lakeview, and Clark Fork Quadrangles show a similar loss of backcountry. As the roads have come, the trails have gone. Where there were once several excellent trail systems, especially on upper Lightning Creek and around Packsaddle Mountain, there are now many scattered fragments. Most remaining trails either follow ridgelines with clearcuts below, or valleys with clearcuts above. Long hikes are scarce, and most, like the Alpine, Pend Oreille Divide, or Independence Creek Trails, involve open-ended "loops".

One might ask what multiple use benefits have come from this development. Well, logging has certainly benefited. In a few cases, mining has also been helped. Wildlife benefits have long ago reached a point of diminishing returns, and elk (like people) are running out of the quiet places they need. Water quality has certainly been hurt by the huge clearcuts of the past. So, what of recreation? Of course, dispersed recreation has suffered from closed trails, but have the surviving trails been improved to handle increased traffic? The answer is generally, no. Portions of the Pend Oreille Divide, Alpine, and Coeur d'Alene River Trails have been reconstructed. But many trails in the area are in poor condition and getting worse. And what about the opportunities for developed recreation? Have campgrounds been built in newly accessed areas? Again, the answer is no. There are severe shortages of campsites around Packsaddle Mountain and along Lightning Creek. Campgrounds here would help people walk the many dayhikes that remain from former trail networks.

The roadless areas of the Coeur d'Alene and Clark Fork have vast recreation potential, with an ideal mix of mountain lakes, meadows, ridges, and peaks. The Forest Service should be proud to manage such fine country; it should encourage its use. Yet the author feels the official policy for this resource is one of malign neglect. He strongly doubts whether such a policy can be in the long term interest of Panhandle residents.

36. Coeur d'Alene River

Hikes: D, O, W.
Total Distance, W: 14 miles.
Difficulty: Level I.
Season: March 25 – September 20.
Elevation Gain: 500 feet.
USGS Maps: Jordan Creek,
  Cathedral Peak.
USFS Map: Coeur d'Alene N. F.; or,
  I. P. N. F.
Mileage, CdA: 79 (no dirt).

Introduction: There is too little unspoiled country in the Coeur d'Alene River drainage. This trail's high quality, the excellent campsites and viewpoints it passes, and its easy access mark it as one that must be preserved.

The Trail: Dayhikers and overnighters can choose their own goals on this 7 mile trail. Weekenders can take it easy here or continue up the river past the Jordan Creek Road. The trail has been moved, and now comes just before the new bridge over the Couer d'Alene River. (The old trailhead across the river is still signed.) This new trail briefly climbs before descending to a flat where you may camp. It then meets a remarkable rocky spur that forces the river to turn and the trail to climb. From this vantage you can see the old trail. The new descends to meet the old, but it continues to stay well above the river. An early vista embraces the majestic Cataract Creek Gorge, a canyon that merits exploration. As you continue along the trail you pass above several large, flat gravel bars that become more heavily forested as you go north. These and other bars offer excellent camping. Cathedral Rocks is the last major view. A mile beyond is the ford of Jordan Creek and the Jordan Creek Road.

Extensions: You could cross Jordan Creek, and continue north to Alden Creek.

Access: Take I-90 from Coeur d'Alene Junction to Kingston (Exit 43) and turn left on the paved Coeur d'Alene River Road. Follow the road to the Wallace junction and then continue north for 26½ miles. There are several campgrounds along the road, and campsites ½ mile down the trail.

37. Independence Creek

Hikes: D, O, W, E.
Total Distance, W: 16 miles.
Difficulty: Level II.
Season: June 25 – September 20.
Elevation Gain: 800 feet.
USGS Maps: Cathedral Peak,
  Lakeview (1:62,500).
USFS Map: Coeur d'Alene N. F.; or,
  I. P. N. F.
Mileage, CdA: 85 (5½ dirt).

Introduction: Independence Creek drains a large roadless area which was not always roadless: at one time a wagon road followed the creek. Its remains have largely vanished, and now only the trail endures. It crosses the creek sixteen times, and although the Forest Service advises you to wear heavy boots, a pair of sneakers might be better! A fair quality trail, with lots of fords: Level II.

The Trail: Overnighters can find campsites in the flats past Minor Creek, 2 miles in; weekenders can make 15 fords and camp 8 miles in near the Snowbird Road; dayhikers can follow their whims. Start with an atypical climb that avoids a pair of crossings, descend to Trident Creek, and climb again. A long mile on the north bank is followed by the first crossing. There is good camping around Green Creek, where you again cross to the north bank, thus avoiding a big washout. From Snow Creek to the Snowbird Road there are eleven crossings. On this stretch the trail passes through deep dark forests that are usually too dense to camp in. However, there is a large meadow near the road.

Extensions: All three trails up to Faset Peak, an abandoned lookout, are well marked and look good. The best campsites further up the creek are near Declaration and Camp Creeks.

Access: Follow directions above, except drive 4¾ miles past the trailhead to the Independence Creek Road. Turn right, then bear left. Go 1 mile to the trailhead, where you can camp. There are campsites ½ mile in.

The incredible outcrop

The view from mid-ford

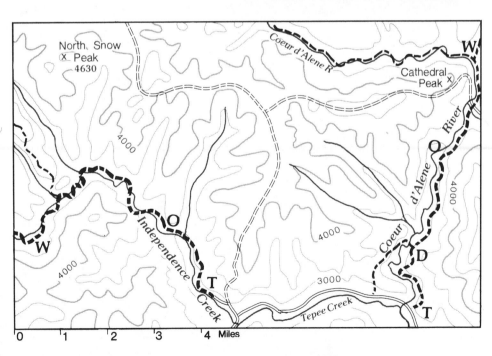

38. Mount Pend Oreille

Hikes: D, O, W.
Total Distance, O: 7 miles.
Difficulty: Levels I, III.
Season: July 1 – September 20.
Elevation Gain: 1900 feet.
USGS Map: Mt. Pend Oreille (1:62,500).
USFS Map: Kaniksu N. F.; or,
    I. P. N. F.
Mileage, CdA: 72 (14 dirt).

Introduction: A number of trails lead to high peaks and lakes from the head of Lightning Creek. The king of these mountains, the highest peak between the Clark Fork and Kootenai Rivers, is Mt. Pend Oreille, 6755. The trail to Lake Darling is Level I, but from there to the Divide Trail and down Gordon Creek trails are steep, rocky, poorly maintained, unsigned, and hard to follow: Level III.

The Trail: Hikes here, like elsewhere in the area, are either day or overnight hikes. Lake Darling is an easy 2 miles in; Mt. Pend Oreille is 5 miles in, and a loop over 6628, just south of Mt. Pend Oreille, is 7½ miles long. The first stretch of trail follows an old road. A ways past Gordon Creek you see another old road going left. This is the Gordon Creek Trail. Most of the level ground your map shows on the way to Lake Darling is either brushy or boggy and there just aren't any established campsites. The lake itself, with its fine view of Mt. Pend Oreille, shows heavy impact. Some campers the author met were shooting off firecrackers and wondering why the moose went away! Not recommended for camping unless you carry your machete and hack out a spot in the brush away from the lake.

As soon as you leave the lake the trail deteriorates. It passes through bogs on its way to an avalanche-scarred area at 5400 feet. You could eke out a campsite here, as the soil is thick and the brush thin. From here the trail bears a bit to the right and climbs a grassy slope. A rocky climb to the left brings you to a large camping area just below the ridgeline. From there you can

make the climb north to Mt. Pend Oreille. A challenging loop would go east from the summit and follow the ridge to the Callahan Creek Trail (which seems to be there).

The Gordon Creek loop goes south from the camping area. After a steep stony climb you pass some good ridgeline campsites and then come to a nice new contouring trail that avoids the ridgetop. The new trail rounds the south side of the ridge to the left, and switches back to the right. It meets the Gordon Creek Trail in a few minutes. While unsigned, the trail divide is faily obvious: watch for the trail cutting back and down to the left. There is a reasonably reliable spring just 100 feet down this trail. As your USGS map shows, the Gordon Creek Trail stays on the hillside all the way down to Lightning Creek. Along the way it offers good chances to observe wildlife in the valley below.

Extensions: There are other day and overnight hikes nearby, in the Moose and Gem Lake areas. You can also start at Lunch Peak Lookout and hike north past Mt. Pend Oreille.

Access: Drive 45½ miles north of Coeur d'Alene Junction and turn right on ID-200. Go 12½ miles on ID-200 to the Trestle Creek Road. Turn left and drive 13 miles to the Lightning Creek Road. Turn left and drive 1 mile to a "Trail 52" sign. There is no camping at the trailhead or on the trail for 2 miles; there are some campsites along Lightning Creek south of the Trestle Creek Road.

Darling Lake and Mt. Pend Oreille

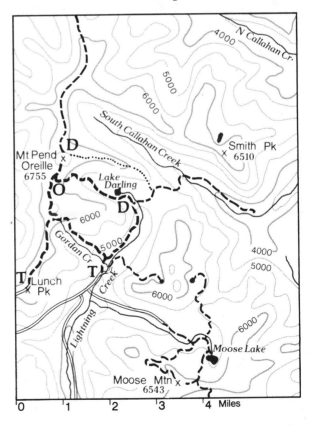

39. The Alpine Trail

Hikes: D, O, W.
Total Distance, O: 12 miles.
Difficulty: Levels I, II.
Season: June 25 – September 20.
Elevation Gain: 1200 feet.
USGS Maps: Mt. Pend Oreille,
   Clark Fork (Both 1:62,500).
USFS Map: Kaniksu N. F.; or,
   I. P. N. F.
Mileage, CdA: 68 (9½ dirt).

Introduction: This trail is also known as the "Roundtop-Beetop Divide Trail", or as the "120 Trail." It is 20½ miles long, with exciting scenery all the way. A "bonus" trailhead in the middle makes for a variety of hiking opportunities. Limiting these is a lack of good water and good campsites, so trail use is restricted to day and overnight hiking. Near the two high trailheads hiking is easy, Level I; elsewhere along the trail things are Level II.

The Trail: Dayhikers and overnighters can go south from either the Trestle Creek or Wellington Creek Roads. Weekenders have two choices, to make an open-ended loop hiking all 20½ miles, or to start at Wellington Creek or Clark Fork and hike the six miles to water and camping. From Trestle Creek Pass, the trail makes a lazy switchback climb to the saddle north of Trestle Peak. It crosses several streams, with the ones at 5500 feet offering the last water on the eight mile stretch to Wellington Creek. Campsites here, as elsewhere on the 120 Trail, are dry ridgetop ones, mostly in uneven bunchgrass. Trestle Peak itself, 2½ miles in, would make a good dayhiker's goal. Past there the trail becomes more rocky, and it has some steep stretches under Round Top Mountain. To pick up this northern section of trail from the Wellington Creek Road, go north a very short distance on a poor road and take the trail that heads left.

The trail immediately south of the road is of the highest quality – one place where the Forest Service *has* mitigated recreation resource losses in the area. It gently climbs to a saddle, an excellent dayhiker's goal, where the view encompasses beautiful Wellington Creek to the east and beautiful Lake Pend Oreille to the west. The trail relentlessly contours to the next saddle, where there is some camping. Just five minutes past here is a small spring, the main water source on the southern trail segment. There is more camping at the *next* saddle, where you can view Porcupine Lake. The new trail then goes south, then north on a ridge, then east (good campsites here). And then it ends momentarily, until you meet the old, adequate trail. Past here you see the trail that descends to Porcupine Creek, which looks very, very steep. Your route to the Beetop Trail divide continues as mapped. You can camp here. The descent to Clark Fork is surprising, for the trail is excellent, with the right number of switchbacks to yield a good grade. There's lots of shade, water at 3800 feet, and a waterfall just off the trail near the bottom.

Extensions: You could start at Clark Fork and hike almost to the Kootenai using the Alpine Trail, the road to Lunch Peak Lookout, the Pend Oreille Divide Trail, and the Boulder and Buck Mountain Trails.

Access: From three places. Drive north on ID-95 from Coeur d'Alene Junction for 45½ miles, to ID-200, and go east on ID-200. After 12½ miles turn left on the Trestle Creek Road. Climb 9½ miles to Trestle Creek Pass, the trailhead, where there is camping. For Wellington Creek, drive 13 miles further on ID-200 to Clark Fork, and turn left on the Lightning Creek Road. Drive about 12 miles on Lightning Creek to the Wellington Creek/Auxor Mine Road, and turn left. Follow the main road to the pass, where there is a little camping. For the southern trailhead, drive east on ID-200 to the fish hatchery road just before Clark Fork. Turn left and drive 2¼ miles up this road, then turn right (at the first road to the right). After a long ½ mile turn left, and after ¾ mile, at a "T" intersection, turn right and then immediately bear left on a small road. The trailhead is ¼ mile ahead, with camping.

Upper Wellington Creek

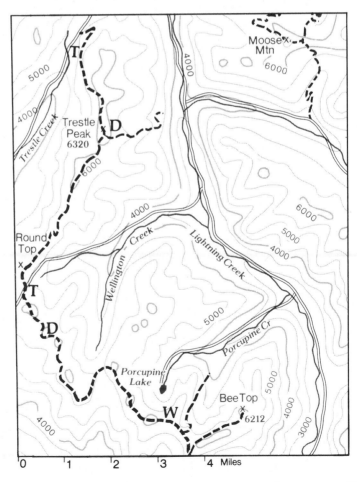

40. Packsaddle Mountain

Hikes: D, O.
Total Distance, O: 5 miles.
Difficulty: Levels I, II, III.
Season: June 1 – September 20.
Elevation Gain: 1900 feet.
USGS Map: Packsaddle Mtn. (1:62,500).
USFS Map: Coeur d'Alene N. F.; or,
   I. P. N. F.
Mileage, CdA: 89 (17½ dirt).

Introduction: Roads have replaced many trails in the Packsaddle area. But the endless view from Packsaddle Mountain, the ageless forest of Granite Creek, and the ruthless descent down Minerva Ridge still reward hikers. The Granite Creek Trail, for its first two miles, is so gentle it could be hiked in moccasins (Level I); the Packsaddle Mountain Trail presents minor route-finding problems (Level II); while the Minerva Ridge Trail is steep, rocky, and hard to follow (Level III).

The Trails: The Granite Creek Trail is a *pleasant* trail, a perfect dayhike, easy on the feet and on the soul. Start by the sign 100 yards past Granite Creek, and you are soon on an old trail that once ran from Lake Pend Oreille to Packsaddle Mountain. A dense cedar forest keeps the creek well in earshot but just out of eyesight, and contributes a dense layer of needles to the trail. After two miles you reach an old cabin site, where you can camp if you don't mind ghosts. Past here the trail crosses Granite Creek on a log and changes character, climbing a rocky stretch. From a brushy hillside further on you can view Packsaddle's rugged north flank. At last you come to Trail 611, which you descend to the creek. The cedar forest there is very nice.

The Packsaddle Mountain Trail is as steep as the Granite Creek Trail is level. It makes short work of a 1900 foot climb to the old lookout site. Go down the logging road fifty feet to the trail sign, and start your climb. It will take you through a changing environment of trees, boulders, and grasses. When you enter the grasses the trail becomes hard to follow. It generally zigs and zags toward the northeast end of the mountain's broad summit. It then cuts back to the left and the peak, where you could make a dry camp. The trail is not snow free until mid-June.

The Minerva Ridge Trail is the most challenging and the longest of this trio. Good views of the lake quickly reward the climb from the trailhead. Once on top of the ridge, you proceed through lush grand fir forests. Leave the forest to climb directly up to 5408, as shown on the map. From the signed junction with Trail 611, you climb in earnest. On passing the unsigned Falls Creek Trail junction you can look down into the Packsaddle cirque. At the next trail divide, ½ mile farther, go left on the final climb to Packsaddle Mountain. Dry camping is possible in grand fir and lodgepole pine stretches of the trail, and at the summit. Open as far as Trail 611 by June 1; above there you may meet snow until July 1.

Access: Easiest access is via Clark Fork. Drive north on US-95 to ID-200. Go straight on ID-200 25¾ miles to Clark Fork, and turn right at the National Forest Access sign. Cross the old bridge and turn right. After 9¼ miles you come to the junction with Road 278, at the top of the ridge. For Packsaddle Mountain, turn left and drive 3½ miles to another junction, where you turn right on the Pend Oreille Divide Road. Drive 4 miles and turn right on the Scenic Drive Road that leads to the trailhead. The nearest established campground is over 35 miles distant. To reach the Minerva and Granite Creek Trails, turn right at Road 278. After 9¾ miles you cross Granite Creek and meet the trailhead. Another 6 miles on Road 278 bring you to the Falls Creek Road junction. Turn left, and after 1/10 mile turn left again, on an old road. After ¼ mile there is a big mining scar on the right, where you can park. Past here the road is very rough. The unsigned Minerva Ridge trailhead is about 100 yards down the road. You can car camp on USFS land bordering the Falls Creek Road.

Clouds over the Coeur d'Alene country

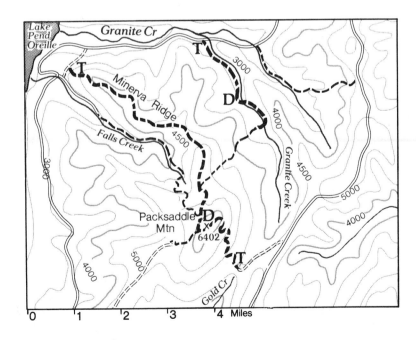

41. Scotchman Peak

Hikes: D, O.
Total Distance: 10 miles.
Difficulty: Level II.
Season: June 25 – September 20.
Elevation Gain: 3700 feet.
USGS Map: Clark Fork (1:62,500).
USFS Maps: Kaniksu N. F.; or,
  I. P. N. F.
Mileage, CdA: 77½ (6 dirt).

Introduction: The Greek philosopher Parmenides felt that man's senses were so imperfect that he could not make any meaningful comment about reality; that the only true statement one could make was: "It is." When you hike the Scotchman Peak Trail, your senses will all agree with the reality that "It is up." This is not a typical weekend backpacking trip, but rather a day hike/climb. Scotchman Peak soars 5000 feet above the Clark Fork River, and from its summit you can gaze south to the Coeur d'Alene River Peaks, west to Lake Pend Oreille and the Selkirks, north to the Pend Oreille Divide, and east to the Cabinet Mountains. RARE-II honored the beauty and ruggedness of this area with a wilderness recommendation. The trail is occasionally steep and rocky; Level II.

The Trail: Scotchman Peak is about 5 miles in and ¾ miles up. There are some spots along the trail suitable for dry camping, but otherwise this is a day hike. Your USFS map is of little value on this hike, except to aid your compass work from the top. The USGS map is very accurate, surprisingly so considering its 1951 date. You start your hike with 600 feet of very steep climbing, just as shown on the USGS map. The first switchback then appears, and more follow to ease your way up another 500 feet of

mountain. You then climb up a long steep ridgeline stretch, which is followed by a series of gentle switchbacks along an open slope with good views of Lake Pend Oreille. This area makes a good stopping point.

Just above a campsite at 6500 feet, you enter a world of rock. From here on the route is marked by cairns. At one tricky spot you make a left turn and contour to the very north edge of the ridge. The final stretch of ridgeline trail stays to the right, and the climb to the summit begins just above an old hut. The lookout is unusual; most such abandoned structures are burned by the Forest Service.

Extensions: A different route to Scotchman Peak climbs the Goat Mountain Trail. It is the very steepest trail in all Idaho, too steep to safely descend. The non-trailed stretch over the saddle between Goat and Scotchman is easy.

Access: Drive north from Coeur d'Alene Junction to the junction of US-95 and ID-200, 1 mile north of Sandpoint. Go straight on ID-200 for 25½ miles, to the Lightning Creek Road in Clark Fork. Turn left, and after ¾ mile turn right on the Mosquito Creek Road. After 3 more miles turn left, and the trailhead appears shortly. You can car camp near the trailhead; the first campsite on the trail is 3000 feet up.

The old lookout

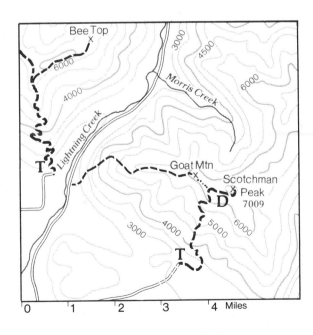

42. Black Peak

Hikes: D, O, W.
Total Distance, W: 14 miles.
Difficulty: Levels I, II.
Season: June 25 – September 20.
Elevation Gain: 2600 feet.
USGS Maps: Burke, Cooper Gulch
  (both 1:62,500).
USFS Map: Coeur d'Alene N. F.
Mileage, CdA: 70 (12½ dirt).

Introduction: This is the longest remaining section of the State Divide Trail north of Lookout Pass, and development is beginning to close in on it. West Eagle Creek is protected by the Settler's Grove of Ancient Cedars at its lower end, but threatened by mining at its upper end. Clearcuts on the new Cottonwood Creek Road are getting closer to the trail and are very much in the "seen area." At any rate, this is a fine trail, well marked and maintained, that offers excellent mountain hiking and lakeside or ridgeline camping. The first stretch is Level I; access to lakes is Level II.

The Trail: Your goal is East Lake, 7 miles in. Dayhikers can climb Black Peak, 4 miles in, while overnighters have several possibilities past Black Peak or along the ridge about 5 miles in. Start with a full canteen. The trail begins by climbing gently, with occasional switchbacks. It then contours along the rocky mountainside, and skirts the southwest side of Black Peak, passing some springs. The only clearly marked route to the summit leaves from the saddle to the west of the mountain. From here, too, a signed trail leads down the East Fork Trout Creek. And finally, if you drop down from here and contour to the left, you will find campsites northnorthwest of 5855.

The Casper Creek trail is signed. It comes after a climb and just beyond an elegant meadow. Past here, on the top of the Section 35 ridge, there are good dry campsites. The East Lake turnoff comes at a rocky saddle, just before the barren peak at 6130. There are many campsites there, and more at Berry Lake. To reach Berry, climb up the rugged hillside *before* you start to descend by switchbacks, and then cross-country on down to the lake. From here to the Attebury Creek Road, the trail is in good condition.

Extensions: You can continue on down West Eagle Creek to Settlers Grove. The trail is in wretched condition, unmaintained in many a year. Turn left at the Attebury Creek Road and walk about 2 miles to a three-way junction, take the signed West Eagle Trail (a road), and descend to a mine on the creek. Cross the bridge, turn right, and watch to your right for a route that crosses the creek just before some beaver ponds. This is the trail! There is no camping on the way to Settler's Grove, and virtually no trail, either.

Access: Drive east on I-90 to Exit 43, Kingston. Turn left and follow the Coeur d'Alene River Road 23½ miles to the second Pritchard Road, where you turn right. Go 2½ miles and turn left on the East Eagle Road. At the Jack Waite mine the road narrows and steepens, but it should be passable for most cars. The trailhead is at the summit. You can camp there or at a lonely clearcut 1½ miles down the trail and to the right.

Black Peak

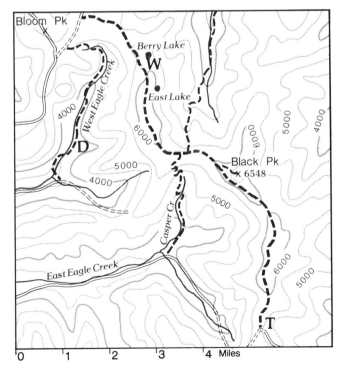

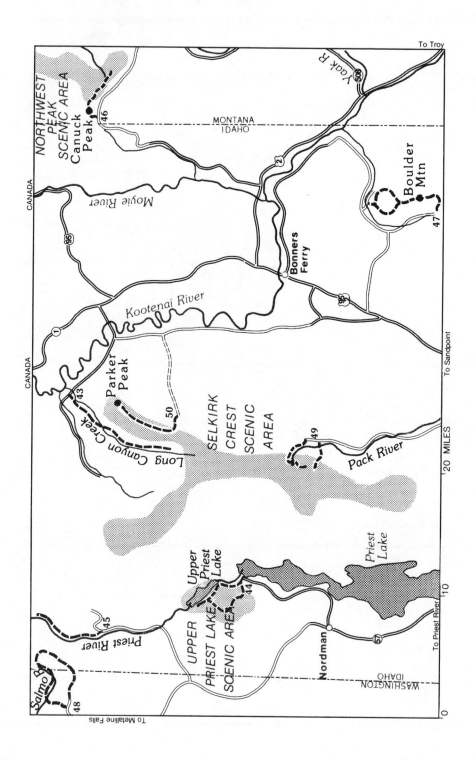

Map labels (rotated):

To Troy

Yaak R.

NORTHWEST PEAK SCENIC AREA

Canuck Peak

46

MONTANA
IDAHO

Boulder Mtn

47

2

Moyie River

CANADA

95

Bonners Ferry

95

Kootenai River

1

CANADA

Parker Peak

43

50

SELKIRK CREST SCENIC AREA

Long Canyon Creek

49

Pack River

To Sandpoint

20 MILES

Priest Lake

Upper Priest Lake

UPPER PRIEST LAKE SCENIC AREA

44

45

Priest River

Nordman

5

To Priest River

10

WASHINGTON
IDAHO

Salmo

48

To Metaline Falls

0

104

Selkirk and Kootenai

The very tip of the Idaho Panhandle contains some of the state's most inspiring scenery. The majestic Kootenai River flows into the state from Canada via Montana, and exits back into Canada to meet the Columbia. The Yaak and Moyie Rivers and Boulder Creek, major tributaries to the Kootenai, drain exciting alpine areas. To the west of the Kootenai rises the Selkirk Range, 250 miles long, which begins near Sandpoint and continues far north into Canada. Priest River drains the western flank of the Selkirks and the Snowy Top area. As long as men love mountains, people will visit these to hike, camp, and contemplate.

The future of this great resource is in doubt. RARE-II recommended wilderness protection for the Selkirk Crest and Salmo-Priest areas; "further planning" for Long Canyon, Parker, and Smith Creeks in the northern Selkirks, and for the Priest Lake Scenic Area; and non-wilderness for the Northwest Peak Scenic Area. The last area, plus Boulder Mountain, will probably continue as they are—typical I.P.N.F. high country ridges with clearcuts ever advancing up their slopes. The Long Canyon area is fully deserving of wilderness protection. Its environment is unmarred by the sights and sounds of logging; its timber values are suspect, given the cost of building roads on such steep granitic terrain; the recreational opportunities are outstanding; and the area is large enough and diverse enough to be managed as wilderness. The Salmo-Priest area around Snowy Top is also a must for wilderness classification. It shelters Idaho's (and the lower forty-eight states') only caribou herd. Even in Idaho, a state full of wonders, its incredible variety, from the cedars of the Upper Priest River to the snowfields on Snowy Top's north face, make it special. And, its environment includes a healthy dose of spectacular views. The Southern Selkirks around the Pack River are perhaps less deserving of wilderness protection. The narrow tract of Forest Service land there is probably better suited to its current Scenic Area management. This designation allows more flexibility in recreation planning than does wilderness. For the same reasons, the Upper Priest Lake Scenic Area with its campground facilities might best remain as is. It must be stressed that none of these areas is currently wilderness, that the recommendations of RARE-II do not *have* to be acted on, and that without citizen awareness of these areas and action in their behalf, they won't be.

43. Long Canyon

Hikes: D, O, W, E.
Total Distance, W: 18 miles.
Difficulty: Levels I, II.
Season: June 10—September 20.
Elevation Gain: 3100 feet.
USGS Maps: Smith Falls, Smith Peak,
  Shorty Peak*.
USFS Maps: Kaniksu N. F.; or,
  I. P. N. F.
Mileage, CdA: 104½ (no dirt).

Introduction: Long Canyon is the key to the Panhandle's biggest wilderness, one that ranges from 1800 feet where Canyon Creek meets the Kootenai flats to 7653 at the summit of Smith Peak. The Long Canyon Trail is not hard to follow, but it does have a difficult ford after five miles. The ford is usually passable in late June, but it can become ugly any time summer storms dump rain on the Selkirk high country. Level I to the ford; Level II thereafter.

The Trail: The dayhiker's goal is the Kootenai River viewpoint, 1 steep mile in. Overnighters must hike 3 miles to reach the first campsites, which are next to the creek and limited in number. Weekenders can hike 9 miles to reach the broad valley of upper Long Canyon. Climb on the trail until you reach a road. Turn left on the road, and then climb to the right on an old road which is becoming trail again. A stream drains the bench behind 2641, and you could camp in this area. Just past here you have your first good views back over the Kootenai Valley.

Soon after, you are deep within the confines of Long Canyon, passing small side creeks and traversing and climbing along the open slopes your USGS map shows. You finally descend to the creek level, where there are a few campsites. More campsites are on both sides of the first ford, which comes after you bear left at the crudely signed, unmaintained Cutoff Peak Trail. While this point may be reached as early as late May, high water and snowbanks on the south side of the creek will prohibit further travel. The next two fords shown on your USGS map aren't there, but the third, at 4000 feet, is there, and it is much easier. Climb to Cutoff Peak Creek, descend a bit, and meet campsites. A half mile beyond you enter the broad, glacial carved upper valley, where there is much more sun than below. There are campsites there, and at Smith Lake Creek, just before the third ford. There are more campsites near the junction with the Pyramid Pass Trail.

Extensions: You could cross-country up to Cutoff or Smith Lake, or you could climb the Pyramid Pass Trail. The trail over Long Canyon Pass into the upper Smith Creek area has been cleared as far as the Kent Creek divide. One crucial point on it is misrepresented on your USGS map: the trail doesn't use what the map calls Long Canyon Pass. It instead crosses the pass *southwest* of 6921.

Access: Drive north on US-95 from Coeur d'Alene Junction to the junction of US-95 and ID-1. Turn left on ID-1 and drive 1 mile to the Copeland Bridge road. Turn left, go down the hill, and go straight after 1 mile. After crossing the bridge turn right on the Westside Road. The trailhead is 6¾ miles away. The first campsites on the trail would be the marginal ones behind 2641, a mile in. There is an unpardonable lack of car camping sites in this area.

Long Canyon side creek

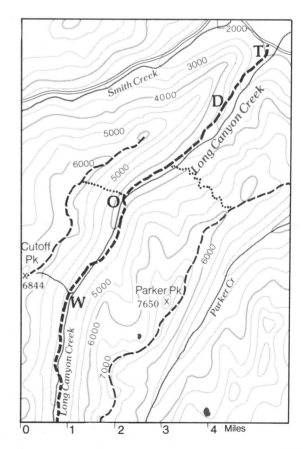

44. Upper Priest Lake

Hikes: D, O, W.
Total Distance, W: 15 miles.
Difficulty: Levels I, III.
Season: May 1 – September 20.
Elevation Gain: 2500 feet.
USGS Maps: Upper Priest Lake,
   Priest Lake NE*.
USFS Map: Kaniksu N. F.; or,
   I. P. N. F.
Mileage, CdA: 99½ (¼ dirt).

Introduction: The Upper Priest Lake Scenic Area is of national stature, a fact recognized by the Idaho Department of Lands' departure from its usual cowboy philosophy of land management ("The only good forest is a logged one"). They are restricting their logging activities to protect the lake's visual environment. That environment is spectacular: from the lakeside trail you are presented with a panorama of the northern Selkirks, from the Lions Head to Snowy Top. This view only improves as you climb the Plowboy Mountain Trail. (When the author stood atop that mountain, though, he was disappointed with the heavy haze in the area. On returning to his car, he turned on the radio, and the first words he heard were, "Mt. St. Helens erupted at 8:57 this morning...") RARE-II recommended further planning for this area, but because of its small size and the need for flexible management of the lakeshore, Scenic Area status is probably adequate. The trail is Level I to Navigation Campground, and Level III over Plowboy Mountain.

The Trail: Weekenders may stop at Navigation Campground, 6 miles in, or may hike a 15 mile loop over Plowboy Mountain. Overnighters can choose among many good sites from the trailhead to Plowboy Campground, 3 miles in. Day-hikers can stop at Armstrong Meadow, 1½ miles in, or go on to a lake view at Plowboy C. G. The trail starts with a level walk along Beaver Creek, crossing the creek and encountering many campsites. These are of the best type – off in the woods, away from the trail and the creek. When you come to

Armstrong Meadows, go right on the trail, which now skirts the wet areas instead of crossing them. Past the ruins of an old cabin, you descend toward the lake and meet the trail that leads down to Plowboy Campground. From here on, the trail moves along the lakeside at a very fast pace, passing the old Navigation Mine shaft and then climbing to pass some dry but wild campsites. A downhill brings you to the Navigation Campground, which is located on the south side of Deadman Creek. A great windfall devastated the area, which has been partially cleared.

If you think the climb over Plowboy Mountain is the easy 1702-foot jaunt your USGS map shows, you're wrong, for that trail is just a figment of the mapper's imagination. What it really does is this: It climbs along Deadman Creek and comes to a trail divide, where you go left. It then ascends via ever-fainter switchbacks until it finally zigs back into the Deadman Creek drainage to a nice creek. From there it works its way to the 4877 foot summit of Plowboy Mountain, where lie the remains of two old lookouts. The trail begins its descent from there by crossing several open, rocky areas on the spur that drops off to the southeast. It passes a curious pond, an indicator of the wet slope that lower down features such wet environment plants as shooting star, rare on southern exposures. At about 3400 feet the trail meets an old logging road, which it follows for a long mile until meeting the Beaver Creek Road. Turn left at this signed trail-head. The Navigation Trailhead is 2½ miles down the road.

Extensions: The Navigation Trail becomes the Hatchery Trail, and meets the Upper Priest River Road 4 miles past Navigation Campground.

Access: Follow directions for the Upper Priest River Trail, page 110, until you reach Nordman. Then turn right on the Reeder Bay Road. Stay on that paved road until it ends at the Beaver Creek Road. Turn right and then take the first left. The trailhead is ¼ mile further. There is camping along the lake there, and campsites on the trail past Beaver Creek, ½ mile in.

The northern Selkirks from Plowboy Campground

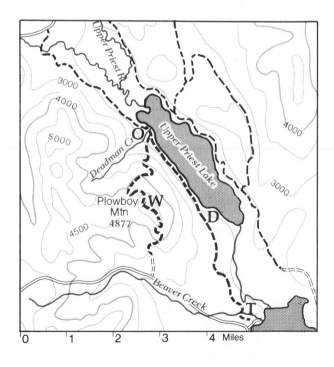

45. Upper Priest River

Hikes: D, O, W, E.
Total Distance, W: 17 miles.
Difficulty: Levels I, II, III.
Season: May 15 — September 20.
Elevation Gain: 700 feet.
USGS Map: Continental Mountain.
USFS Maps: Kaniksu N.F.; or, I.P.N.F.
Mileage, CdA: 113½ (22½ dirt).

Introduction: This is one of Idaho's finest trails, through the state's biggest and most magical cedar forest. For seven miles the trail winds through western red cedar, with the roar of Upper Priest River providing the audio for this marvelous video. The trail encounters a tremendous number of springs, creeks, and bogs, a fact to strike terror in the hearts of hikers who have experienced the infinite drudgery of deep muck trudgery. But put yourself at ease — an outstanding system of boardwalks and bridges gets you across most of the wet spots with dry feet. At the end of the trail lies Upper Priest Falls (known locally as American Falls), a stunning wall of white water. The trail is Level I, fairly flat and easy to follow. Only in its last mile does it become Level II, because the canyon narrows and trail segments have been washed out.

The Trail: Weekenders should find a campsite before they cross Malcolm Creek, 7 miles in, and then dayhike their way to the falls. Overnighters can stop when the spirit moves them — campsites are numerous. And dayhikers can just go until they see faeries and demons in the enchanted forest, at which point they had best turn back. The start is easy to locate, and there is little to say about the trail as far as Malcolm Creek; it stays very well behaved. Highlights are the signed Little Snowy Top Trail junction and the occasional views you get of that and other high peaks to the west.

When you reach the campsites at Malcolm Creek, though, something does happen. Something bad. The glory days of the trail come to an end, and it finally makes you work. The river is jealous of American Falls, and it has washed out the trail to try and protect it from prying eyes. The result is a pair of steep, rocky, slippery detours. After the second one you hike along the base of a rocky streambank, turn a corner, and confront the falls.

Extensions: Your USGS map shows the trail continuing on into Canada. This trail is extraordinarily challenging — steep, unblazed, unmaintained in many a year, and rarely travelled. Try it! You could also take the Little Snowy Top trail on its switchbacking 3200 foot climb to the ridge above (see The Salmo Loop, page 116).

Access: Drive west on I-90 from Coeur d'Alene Junction to Exit 7, ID-41, and go north towards Rathdrum. Follow ID-41 until it ends in Oldtown at US-2. Go right on US-2 for 6 miles to ID-57 in Priest River. Turn left and drive to Nordman, 37 miles. Go straight at Nordman and follow the Granite Creek Road to its junction with the Nordman-Metalline Road, 14¾ miles further. Bear right there and continue for 11½ miles, until you see the trail sign. You can car camp at Granite Falls or Muskegon Lake, or near the trailhead by the road or trail.

American Falls

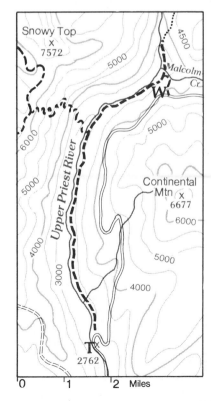

46. Canuck Peak

Hikes: D, O, W, E.
Total Distance, O: 11 miles.
Difficulty: Levels II, III.
Season: July 4 – September 20.
Elevation Gain: 2000 feet.
USGS Maps: Canuck Peak,
   Northwest Peak (Mont.).
USFS Map: Kootenai N.F.
Mileage, CdA: 144½ (13 dirt).

Introduction: The northeastern boundary of the Kaniksu N.F. swings into Montana, leaving Idaho at Line Point and following the divide between the Moyie and Yaak Rivers. South of Canuck Pass much of that high country divide burned in 1931. North of the pass lies a region of high rocky peaks that the USFS has set aside as the Northwest Peak Scenic Area. Views from these high peaks take in some 200 miles of the Continental Divide to the east, and the entire Selkirk Range to the west. The trail to Canuck Peak is in only fair, Level II condition; the faint trail to the West Fork Yaak and the climb to Ewing Peak are Level III.

The Trail: Canuck Peak is an easy 4 mile, Ewing Peak a tough 9 mile dayhike. The head of the West Fork Yaak is about 5½ miles in, a good overnighter's goal. Intrepid weekenders could follow the divide north to the lake at 6775. The trail to Canuck Peak has character. It is being reclaimed by the hillside, and it tilts a lot, but it is easy to follow, generally doing what your USGS map shows. At the old summit cabin you have choices. You can go south and back; north to American Mountain, on an alleged trail; or east on an unmapped but distinct trail. This trail drops to the 6540 foot level and meets an old sign for the "American Creek Trail No. 1." While it certainly doesn't still reach Canada, it should pass the meadow northeast of Canuck. After descending east to the saddle at 6340, you meet another "ghost" trail, this one headed south. It descends to the top of the clearcut

shown on your map (centered on 5799), then disappears. From the saddle the "main" trail now heads southeast, and contours under Ewing. Just before it emerges from forest to open slope, southsoutheast of Ewing, it passes a good creek – the trail's first water. This open slope is easy to climb, and you can reach the beautiful ridge and then continue up the rocks to the summit and the sublime. You can go down the ridge to the west of Ewing and, when you wish, descend through the brush to meet the trail. Florence Lake, which you see to the right, is too boggy for camping and too shallow for fishing.

To reach the West Fork Yaak, continue on the contouring trail from the open slope past the creek. At the saddle not far beyond, you can cut left into a beautiful valley and camp.

Extensions: If you make it to Ewing's summit, you can make it north over Davis Mountain to Northwest Peak (but expect snow until August 1). Rock Candy Mountain, to the southeast, also looks enticing.

Access: There are two access routes, and you can make a loop of them. The best goes 80½ miles north of Coeur d'Alene Junction to US-2, and turns right. After 7 miles you pass Deer Creek Road, but go straight another 12 miles to MT-508. Turn left, and after 22 miles turn left on the Spread Creek Road. The trailhead is at the pass, 13 miles up. You can exit through Idaho via the Deer Creek Road, but its last 2 miles to the trailhead are very rough.

North of Ewing Peak

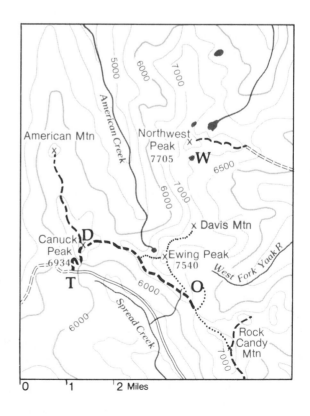

47. Boulder Mountain

Hikes: D, O, W.
Difficulty: Levels I, II+.
Total Distance, W: 14 miles.
Season: July 1 – September 20.
Elevation Gain: 3000 feet.
USGS Maps: Clifty Mtn.
USFS Map: Kaniksu N.F.; or, I.P.N.F.
Mileage, CdA: 86 (17½ dirt).

Introduction: Boulder, Iron, and Buck Mountains anchor the northern end of the Pend Oreille Divide. Although the valleys below them are being logged, their lack of trees will protect them from man's heavy hand. The Middle Fork Boulder Creek Trails are steep and rocky with occasional routefinding problems, tough Level II hikes. Trails from the Callahan Divide are easier, Level I routes.

The Trails: Dayhikers can hike to Boulder Mountain, 3 miles in. Overnighters can hike 4 miles from either trailhead to dry campsites. Weekenders can hike the 14 mile Iron Mountain-Buck Mountain loop or the route from Callahan Divide to 6191. Start the loop hike with a full canteen, and locate the trail on the west side of the Middle Fork, just above a barrow pit. When the valley narrows, the unsigned Iron Mountain Trail climbs to the right. It goes straight up the steep ridgeline, finally veering to the left at a clearing with a structure (as your USGS map shows). Just before the saddle between 5862 and Iron Mountain, you pass a small spring. The first of many campsites on the ridge comes near the junction with the trail that leads to Iron. Descend to the left, and soon you are on the ridge in an area of gray trees, gray rocks, and endless mountains disappearing into a gray haze. The Buck Mountain Trail divide is signed. South of here is a signed spring before 6191, a marvelous pond below it, and an unmapped descent that takes you west of 6092, past some water, and then on to Divide Lake. The Buck Mountain Trail is less steep and easier to descend. It does a rude thing, though, disappearing when it goes west of the high divide. It conveniently reappears at each of the next three saddles, where there are campsites. When you descend to the 4000 foot level, the old trail becomes brushy, and it meets a new trail that descends directly to the new road. The old trail continues down to the barrow pit.

The trail from the Callahan Divide east to Divide Lake is much easier going. The only problem is a lack of use that is letting the grass take over the trail, making it hard to follow as it switchbacks up some open slopes. At about 5600 feet there is a sign indicating water to the left of the trail. Not far beyond is Divide Lake, one of those amazing perched pond/lakes of the Pend Oreille divide which hold water all year. There are several campsites around the lake. If you turn left before the lake, you climb up the ridge toward Boulder Mountain, an easy scramble.

Extensions: Callahan Divide also provides access to the Pend Oreille Divide Trail. From Divide Lake, you can still hike east over Middle Mountain.

Access: Drive 68½ miles north from Coeur d'Alene Junction on US-95, and turn right on the Twentymile Creek Road. Drive 12¼ miles, over Twentymile Pass, to the Boulder Creek Road junction. Turn left for the Middle Fork trailhead. Drive 4¾ more miles to a new road and bridge across Boulder Creek. Turn right, and after ¼ mile turn right again to reach the Iron Mountain trailhead at a barrow pit. That is, if you can reach the barrow pit. Although the Boulder Plan calls the Iron Mountain Trail a "Forest Primary Trail," its first 200 yards were obliterated by a road and barrow pit for timber road construction. And just moving the road and pit 50 feet to the west would have left the trail untouched! If you can't reach this trailhead, use the new Buck Mountain trailhead, about ¼ mile up the new road. To reach the Callahan Divide, turn right from the Boulder Creek Road junction and drive 6¼ miles to the road's end. You can camp at the barrow pit trailhead in the lodgepoles, or on upper Boulder Creek near the bridge. First overnight campsites are 4 miles from the Middle Fork, and 3 miles from the Callahan Divide.

Boulder Mountain from the Callahan Divide Trail

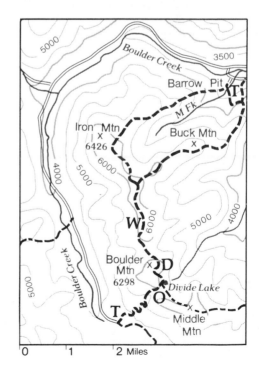

48. The Salmo Loop

Hikes: D, O, W, E.
Total Distance, W: 20 miles.
Difficulty: Levels I, II.
Season: July 10 — September 20.
Elevation Gain: 3000 feet.
USGS Maps: Salmo Mtn,
    Continental Mtn.
USFS Maps: Colville N.F.; or,
    Kaniksu N.F.; or, I.P.N.F.
Mileage, CdA: 106 (20 dirt).

Introduction: Idaho's northwest corner is adorned by Snowy Top, a splendid peak that reaches 7572 feet. Its summit is 1.7 miles from Upper Priest River and 4600 feet above it — a slope that averages over 50%. The mountain is the high point of the proposed Salmo Priest Wilderness, the home of America's only caribou herd. The Salmo Loop takes in most of the highlights of that area's western portion. Most of the loop trail on the Colville N.F. is well maintained and in excellent, Level I condition. Most of the trail on the Idaho Panhandle N.F. is poorly maintained, and in wretched condition: isn't that funny? Level I to the Shedroof Divide Trail and down to the Salmo River; Level II everywhere else.

The Trails: The full 20 mile loop goes east 2 miles to the Shedroof Divide Trail, north 7 miles to Snowy Top saddle, west 6½ miles down the Salmo, and south 3½ miles to the road, where you are 1 mile from your starting point. The loop is so delightful that you won't notice the long distance. Overnighters and dayhikers can descend to the Salmo (3½ miles) or hike to water on the Shedroof Divide (2 miles), with campsites 1 to 2 miles farther. The loop begins at road's end. A new switchbacking trail takes you to the saddle at the end of the low standard road in Section 23, where there is some camping. A good trail continues on to the Shedroof Divide Trail, which runs 22 miles from Snowy Top to the Nordman-Metalline Road. Turn left here, and after ½ mile you cross a stream. After passing some campsites on a ridge to the left, you descend to the trail your map shows switchbacking down to the Salmo. At this upper end, it looks poorly maintained. This junction

marks the border of the Colville N.F. On some stretches of I.P.N.F. trail ahead, the track will be about 4 inches wide, with a 300 foot dropoff to the side. A few minutes after you begin climbing from the 5600 foot saddle, you come to the last sure water on the divide. Some switchbacks then bring you to the Hughes Ridge "Trail," much of which is road. Past here you reach the best part of the loop, with spectacular views southeast to the Selkirks and northwest to British Columbia's Ripple Mountain. There are a few dry campsites on this ridge, notably northeast of 6429. At last you are at a camping area below Snowy Top.

From here the trail cuts back to the left and meets reliable water at 5850 (an area that may hold snow far into July). The descent along the Salmo proceeds much as the map shows. There is a long stretch of gentle slopes from 5700 to 5500 feet, but unfortunately this is brushy country and your campsite *will* be uneven. Salmo Cabin, shown on your USGS maps as a black square just inside the Washington line, offers some good camping. There are more possible campsites as you move through the cedars on your way down to the signed trail junction where you must turn left and cross the Salmo. There are many campsites at the ford. The hike up to the road is as easy a climb as you're likely to find, thanks to a superb trail. You must walk one mile of road to reach your car.

Extensions: You could "walk up" to the summit of Snowy Top. The best route to Boundary Lake (6178, reached by a road from Canada) is to just climb partway up Snowy Top and contour to the west.

Access: Easiest by way of Metalline Falls, Washington. Drive to Newport via I-90 and ID-41, and take WA-20 to WA-31. Go straight north and drive 16¾ miles to the Sullivan Lake Road. Turn right and after 4¾ miles turn left. Follow Sullivan Creek to its source and up to Salmo Pass. The very end of this road is the trailhead. There are campsites along Sullivan Creek, and just up the trail. You can also drive north from Priest River to Nordman, then up Granite Creek to the Nordman-Metalline Road, then over Pass Creek Pass to Sullivan Road.

Snowy Top anchors Idaho's northwest corner

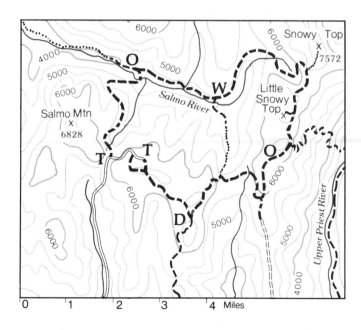

49. Pack River Dayhikes

Hikes: D, O.
Total Distance: 6 miles.
Difficulty: Levels I, II, III.
Season: July 4 – September 20.
Elevation Gain: 1400 feet.
USGS Map: The Wigwams.
USFS Map: Kaniksu N.F.; or,
  I.P.N.F.
Mileage, CdA: 76½ (20½ dirt).

Introduction: The Pack River Valley is one of Idaho's most beautiful places. The Selkirk peaks which bound it have been shaped by glaciers to a perfection unknown in more southerly parts of the state. The USFS recognized this unique beauty by recommending that a Selkirk Crest Wilderness be established. Along the west side of Pack River, the wilderness would vary from ¼ to 2 miles in width. Even with the State of Idaho's limited commitment of lands to scenic area management (extending the maximum width of protected land to 4 miles), can this area be effectively managed as wilderness? Given the fact that the Southern Selkirk Crest trail system currently consists of about 8 dayhikes to mountain lakes, with no connecting trails, shouldn't some alternative to wilderness be considered? Wouldn't huts with outhouses (which wilderness rules prohibit) provide better protection for fragile lakeshores than unlimited *or limited* tent camping? Travel to Harrison Lake is Level I, thanks to reconstruction done by Sierra Club volunteers; travel to Beehive Lakes is Level II; and travel to Little Harrison Lake is Level III cross-country.
The Trails: Harrison Lake is 3 miles in; Beehive Lakes 3½ miles. Both can be day or overnight hikes. Little Harrison Lake is 5 miles in, a long overnighter. The trail to Harrison Lake starts as an old, eroding road. As you climb it you get stunning glimpses of Harrison and other Selkirk peaks. (This must be one of the prettiest spots in all the National Forests: why such a lousy trail?) At about 5660 you cross a creek, see campsites to the left, and meet the good trail. A six hundred foot climb brings you to the lake, where there are many campsites. To reach the meadows above Little Harrison Lake (6271), descend

along the upper Pack River's left bank until it looks like you can turn the corner of the ridge east of 7171. After a bit of a scramble, you climb on glorious granite to the level meadows around 6500 feet. This area can hold snow well into July. Proceed south to the meadow with a spring, shown northwest of the lake. There is no safe route south to Beehive Lakes.

The Beehive Lakes Trail begins with a ford of Pack River. From there, it follows logging roads for 1½ miles. These can be confusing! Just follow the most used, widest, least grassy road and you will soon arrive at Beehive Creek. The crossing here is extraordinarily difficult due to the stream's depth and rockiness. Your best crossing is probably upstream a bit. The trail begins shortly beyond the ford, marked by spraypainted arrows and blazes. This is the wackiest trail in Idaho: when it was built, the trail crew's clinometer must have been broken. Switchbacks go down, up, and down and around. Further up, the trail occasionally disappears while crossing pure granite. The upper lake has good camping. The three-pond cirque basin to the south beckons!
Extensions: A bit of climbing can get you across the Selkirk Crest to the headwaters of Indian Creek.
Access: Drive north on US-95 from Coeur d'Alene Junction to the Pack River Road, 56 miles. Turn left and drive 19¼ miles up the road, to a small side road to the left with a "Trail 279" sign. The Beehive Lakes Trail begins a short distance down this road, at an old bridge site. The Harrison Lake Trail begins 1¼ miles further up the main road. There is a tremendous need for a Forest Service campground on the Upper Pack River, since campsites are very few, mainly at the Beehive trailhead and just up the main road.

Idaho's premiere glacial landscape

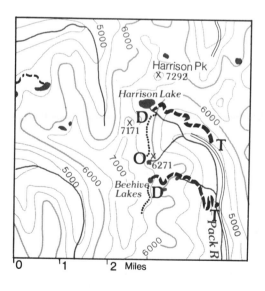

50. Parker Peak

Hikes: D, O, W, E.
Total Distance, W: 16 miles.
Difficulty: Levels II, III.
Season: July 4 – September 20.
Elevation Gain: 3200 feet.
USGS Map: Pyramid Peak.
USFS Map: Kaniksu N.F.; or, I.P.N.F.
Mileage, CdA: 110½ (14 dirt).

Introduction: RARE-II recommended that most of the Forest Service's portion of the Selkirk Crest be made wilderness, and that a large northern area be put in a further planning category. This trail is in that further planning area, and its high quality suggests that perhaps the Forest Service got its recommendations mixed up. Here, as nowhere else in the Selkirks, you get a true sense of wilderness, for here alone can you hike long distances on glorious high ridges without seeing logging roads and logging scars. The key to this area is the Trout Creek trailhead, from which you can go south to Ball Lake, east to Fisher Lake, north to Parker Lake, or west to Long Canyon Creek. The trail is rated Level II as far as Long Mountain Lake due to steep stretches, and Level III thereafter, due to a very faint trail.

The Trail: Dayhikers can stop at Pyramid Pass (or hike to Trout Lake), 3 miles; overnighters can camp just over the pass, or at Long Mountain Lake, 5 miles in; weekenders can go on to the Parker Lake area, 8 miles in. After a gentle climb from the trailhead to the Ball Lake-Trout Lake trail divide, your trail steepens and roughens. When it reaches the Fisher Lake Trail, it passes a small creek, the last water source until the lakes. Turn left there and climb to Pyramid Pass. As you descend off the pass, you meet several campsites to the left. The junction with the trail down to Long Canyon Creek isn't where your USGS map shows, at the low point of the descent from the ridge. Rather, you must first climb 200 feet from that low point to meet the trail.

Keep climbing on a steep trail until you come to the saddle south of Long Mountain, where you have a superb view of Parker Creek's splendid valley. A short climb to the left brings you to the new trail down to Long Mountain Lake. There are many campsites on the ridge just above and before the lake.

To continue on to Parker Lake, stay on the ridgeline past the Long Mountain Lake trail, and you will soon see the trail reappear. It is an exciting trail, one that keeps you on your toes, for it is really only a trace. One important stretch is the west flank of 7445, which it more or less contours along. As it reaches the end of that contour, it switches back to the left to descend to the saddle beyond. Parker Lake soon comes into view. Camping is only fair at the lake: you may prefer to camp on the ridge, and just go down to the lake for water. Parker Peak is an easy walk-up.

Extensions: You could continue down Parker Ridge to the West Side Road, or you could descend to Long Canyon and do the same.

Access: Follow directions for Long Canyon Creek, page 106, except turn *left* when you reach the West Side Road. Drive 4¾ miles and turn right on the Trout Creek Road, which is not for every car! The Forest Service plans to improve it a bit in 1982, but it will probably always be rough and rocky. There are only a few campsites on the way to the trailhead, 9 miles up the road, and none right there. First sites on the trail are over Pyramid Pass, 2 miles in.

Parker Peak and Creek

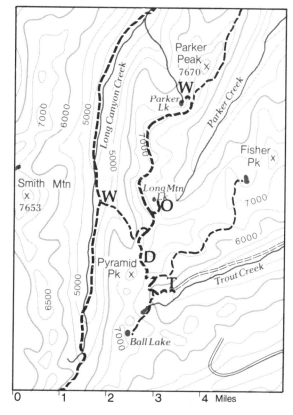

Equipment Checklist

The Ten Essentials

_____USGS and USFS maps
_____Compass
_____Flashlight
_____Extra clothing
_____Sunglasses

_____Waterproofed matches
_____Firestarter
_____Extra food
_____Pocket knife
_____First aid kit

Basics

_____Backpack
_____Tent
_____Sleeping bag
_____Foam pad
_____Rain parka or poncho
_____Insulated parka or vest
_____Wool shirt or sweater
_____Wool hat
_____Bandanna
_____Socks and spare socks
_____Boots
_____Long pants
_____Long-sleeved shirt
_____Stove (filled)
_____Cook kit
_____Ditty bags for food
_____Canteen
_____Food

Extras

_____Day Pack
_____Ground cloth

_____Rain pants
_____Windshirt
_____Gloves or mittens
_____Sun hat
_____Soap and towel
_____Liner socks
_____Moccasins or sneakers
_____Shorts
_____T-shirt
_____Extra fuel container (filled)
_____Grill for fires
_____50 feet of 1/8" nylon cord
_____Collapsible water jug
_____Check the refrigerator!

More Extras

_____Toilet paper
_____Suntan lotion
_____Sewing kit
_____Gaiters
_____Binoculars or monocular
_____Nature guide
_____Toothbrush
_____Candles

_____Insect repellent
_____Ice axe or hiking staff
_____Camera and film
_____Snake bite kit
_____Book
_____Whistle
_____Long johns